Towards Solving the Social Science Challenges

Biljana Mileva Boshkoska (ed.)

Towards Solving the Social Science Challenges with Computing Methods

Bibliographic Information published by the Deutsche Nationalbibliothek
The Deutsche Nationalbibliothek lists this publication in the Deutsche Nationalbibliografie; detailed bibliographic data is available in the internet at http://dnb.d-nb.de.

Library of Congress Cataloging-in-Publication Data

Towards solving the social science challenges with computing methods / Biljana Mileva Boshkoska (ed.). -- 1 Edition.
     pages cm
  ISBN 978-3-631-66018-8
  1. Social sciences--Computer simulation. 2. Social sciences--Mathematical models. I. Boshkoska, Biljana Mileva, 1979- editor.
  H61.3.T693 2015
  300.1'13--dc23
                        2015010223

ISBN 978-3-631-66018-8 (Print)
E-ISBN 978-3-653-05249-7 (E-Book)
DOI 10.3726/ 978-3-653-05249-7

© Peter Lang GmbH
Internationaler Verlag der Wissenschaften
Frankfurt am Main 2015
All rights reserved.
PL Academic Research is an Imprint of Peter Lang GmbH.

Peter Lang – Frankfurt am Main · Bern · Bruxelles · New York · Oxford · Warszawa · Wien

This publication has been peer reviewed.

www.peterlang.com

Acknowledgments

This publication is financed by the Creative Core FISNM-3330-13-500033 'Simulations' project funded by the European Union, The European Regional Development Fund. The operation is carried out within the framework of the Operational Programme for Strengthening Regional Development Potentials for the period 2007–2013, Development Priority 1: Competitiveness and research excellence, Priority Guideline 1.1: Improving the competitive skills and research excellence.

Fakulteta za informacijske študije
Faculty of information studies

Kreativno jedro:
Simulacije
Creative core: Simulations

REPUBLIKA SLOVENIJA
MINISTRSTVO ZA IZOBRAŽEVANJE, ZNANOST IN ŠPORT

Naložba v vašo prihodnost
OPERACIJO DELNO FINANCIRA EVROPSKA UNIJA
Evropski sklad za regionalni razvoj

»Operacijo delno financira Evropska unija in sicer iz Evropskega sklada za regionalni razvoj. Operacija se izvaja v okviru Operativnega programa krepitve regionalnih razvojnih potencialov za obdobje 2007-2013, 1. razvojne prioritete: Konkurenčnost podjetij in raziskovalna odličnost, prednostne usmeritve 1.1: Izboljšanje konkurenčnih sposobnosti podjetij in raziskovalna odličnost.«

"The operation is partially financed by the European Union, mostly from the European Regional Development Fund. Operation is performed in the context of the Operational program for the strengthening regional development potentials for the period 2007-2013, 1st development priorities: Competitiveness of the companies and research excellence, priority aim 1.1: Improvement of the competitive capabilities of the companies and research excellence."

Table of contents

Preface

Computational Social Science is a highly interdisciplinary field in which social science questions are investigated with modern computational tools. This book provides insight into different social problems, which call for the new practices offered by computational social science. It comprises methods for efficient management of complex engineering design, prediction of malicious threads of information systems, and cyber security. It includes topics in awareness of privacy in social networks, prosodic modelling for speech synthesis, and investigates the structure of co-occurrence networks and provides insights into the loosely coupled cloud applications. Another aspect of the field of computing in Social Sciences is envisaged by proposing an extension of synergy models in IMC environment to n-communication channels, and identification and evaluation of knowledge management through information system analysis.

Jana Suklan[1], Vesna Žabkar[2], Nadja Damij[3]
(1) School of Advanced Social Studies in Nova Gorica
Gregorčičeva 19, 5000 Nova Gorica, Slovenia
jana.suklan@fuds.si
(2) Faculty of Economics, University of Ljubljana
Kardeljeva ploščad 17, 1000 Ljubljana, Slovenia
vesna.zabkar@ef.uni-lj.si
(3) Faculty of Information Studies in Novo mesto
Sevno 13, 8000 Novo mesto, Slovenia
nadja.damij@fis.unm.si

Extending Synergy Model in the IMC Environment to n-Communication Channels

Abstract: The presence of synergy represents a key feature in planning marketing activities using integrating marketing communication approach. By combining different multimedia activities, companies are able to benefit from synergy between integrated communication channels. In the presence of synergy, optimal media budget allocation, optimal media mix and advertising carry-over effects differ. The extension of a marketing-mix model provides an insight into how different components of the model interact and elucidate the causes of main and side effects resulting in instant sales and brand awareness over time. In order to understand relationships between different components of the integrated marketing communications model, indicators for four communication channels were integrated into the model. Along with four communication channels an empirical tool for evaluating marketing effectiveness in decision-making processes was developed. Such a tool is very important, since the multichannel marketing environment presents a challenge for marketers and a major source of financial input for companies.

Keywords: Synergy, Carry-over effect, Media Planning, Marketing Integration Model.

1. Introduction

Using market data we calibrated the proposed model to establish the presence of synergy between television and online advertising. Recognizing interaction effects between on-line and off-line activities, we advised managers to consider inter-activity trade-offs in optimally planning marketing-mix strategies (Naik et al. 2005, pp. 2–4). Our focus remained on the extension of the already defined models in the literature that incorporate synergy between media (Naik and Raman 2003, pp. 376) in a manner that meets a specific data collection technique. An article written by Naik and Raman (2003, pp. 383–387) laid the groundwork for the n-media generalisation with differential carryover effect and asymmetric synergy as a future research option. Throughout the analysis, based on detailed collection of reliable proprietary data for each media separately, we intend to contribute to the understanding of consumer response to cross-media strategies.

Marketer's intuitive knowledge must be supported analytically through the development of analytical models to capture the essence of a context and limit the complexity of the model at the same time (Coughlan et al 2010, pp. 3–6). Analysing the data and discussing it with the marketer's increases the understanding of patterns in consumer reactions towards advertising. Throughout the analysis we aimed to understand the relationships and effects of the important indicators in the model.

As Keller (2010, pp. 58) puts it, the challenge for marketers is to choose the right communication options among different for a campaign or business model in order to maximize "push" and "pull" effects in the multimedia environment. Our aim was to include a more complete picture of marketing integration strategy in the previously specified advertising model. We include both direct and indirect channels, and personal and mass communication channels. In terms of channels of distribution, we included on-line as a direct and interactive channel, then resellers (supermarket, catalogue showroom) as an indirect channel. In terms of marketing communications, personal communications were employed through personal selling (company stores) and mass communications through advertising on television.

We define synergy as interaction between communications mixed media targeted at the same market segments aiming to increase the effectiveness of each media due to the presence of the other (Prasad and Sethi 2009, pp. 602). When adding channels to the model we allow the presence of negative effects, if cross-media results in the sum turn out to be less than the individual parts. The negative synergy is connected to cross-media cannibalization when consumer exposure to one media occurs at the expense of the other (Assael 2011, pp. 49) or when one media is taken as a substitute for another, which could lead to cannibalization of one channel by another (Kollmann et al. 2012, pp. 186–194). There is no cross-media cannibalization: while simultaneous usage of media is widespread, it is limited (Enoch and Johnson 2010, pp. 132).

Our paper concentrates on cannibalization in lagged usage, sequential reduction of media usage due to previous usage of other media channels.

A distinction was made due to directionality of synergy, between simultaneous and sequential (Assael 2011, pp. 42–58). In our model we apply both: simultaneous synergy in terms of multi-tasking or simultaneous media consumption of the participating audiences and sequential synergy when we have interaction between media consumption and actual purchase of the product through a chosen channel.

Dealing with synergy we could identify two main streams of research, one analysing data on individual consumer level Havlena et al. (2007, pp. 216) and the other applying models on aggregated data (Naik and Raman 2003, pp. 375–388; Naik and Peters, 2009, pp. 288–299).

Synergy emerges when we accept the fact that channels are inter-correlated and we encourage marketing activities to be aligned in order to maximize the end results. The purpose of IMC is to manage all marketing activities that impact sales, profits, and brand equity simultaneously. The commonly known IMC model emphasizes the role of the joint effects or synergies generated due to the synchronization of multiple activities (Raman and Naik 2006, pp. 381–395).

Advertising models and marketing-mix models are closed-loop solutions. Closed-loop models are symmetric in regard to parameters. Each advertising channel has an input in the channel and output measured in revenue. Such models enable us to understand the role of synergy on the optimal advertising budgeting and allocation of the funds (Prasad and Sethi 2009, 601–610). At the first stage, closed-loop solutions helped us with a budgetary problem definition for two communication channels. We were able to determine the optimal allocation between television and the Internet, with the presence of synergy and the carry-over effect of sales (Prasad and Sethi 2009, pp. 602–603).

However, in order to preserve parsimony in a more complex model we need to retain only the important variables and interactions in the model.

2. Data and methods

In this section, we describe the data set and present parameter estimation results. While adapting the models to the data we check for the existence and implications of the synergy between channels. In order to maintain confidentiality, we rescaled the proprietary time-series data.

The advertising dataset for the chosen brand comprises a weekly time series, starting from the year 2008 to the year 2012. Input data for television advertising consist of a number of commercial minutes (for advertising on air) purchased for public and commercial television stations on the national market, whereas on-line activities are expressed as a number of on-line visitors. Visits represent the number of individual sessions initiated by all the visitors to the Internet site. Input data for a company store is a number of stores opened in the observation period, while input in wholesale is presented by a loyalty scheme of the supermarkets/resellers (dummy variable). The sales data consist of television, on-line, wholesale (reseller) and retail (company stores) sales measured in value of units sold.

We constructed dummy variables to capture seasonal effects of sales; we identified drops (in March and August) and peaks (in December). We apply empirical information from marketers in this product category about advertising decay and its effect on sales using a two-week time lag for the "advertising carry-over" effect.

In the model we include the number of commercial minutes (for advertising on air) for TV advertising, the number of on-line visitors, the number of own retail outlets (stores) and the presence of a loyalty scheme in the supermarket strategy. Additionally, we apply lag revenue on television, Internet, wholesale and retail, followed by simultaneous and sequential synergies. These represent moderating effects of current advertising on carryover effect. Covariates in the model represent seasonal peaks and drops of sales.

The analysis consists of time series data. Regression analysis was run using time series variables. Residuals with time series structure violate the assumption of independent errors in OLS regression; thus we built a model with auto-correlated errors. However, we start the analysis by ordinary least square regression in order to identify an auto-regressive (AR) and moving-average (MA) processes. The structure of the residuals from a linear model is evident from auto-correlation functions (ACF) and partial auto-correlation functions (PACF). PACF helps us to identify an AR process, while we check ACF in order to identify an MA process. We fit the model by using Generalized least square model gls() in the 'nlme' package in R. By standardisation we overcome the problem of different measurement scales. We apply generalized least squares (GLS) regression to our model, because with time-series it is implausible to assume that errors are independent. GLS extends the ordinary least-squares (OLS) estimation of the normal linear model by providing for possible unequal error variances and for correlations between different errors (Weisberg and Fox 2010, pp. 2).

Since a parsimonious model is the desired end result, we must be very thoughtful in regard to which main effects and interactions to include in the model. From a larger set of predictors we select a subset of predictor variables (see Table1) by performing a stepwise selection procedure (both forward and backward) selecting the best model based on the least Aikake Information Criterion (AIC) value (Kabacoff 2011, pp. 208). Such a procedure eliminates some variables from the model.

Here we distance ourselves from OLS regression and introduce AIC as an estimate of the relative distance between the unknown true likelihood function of the data and the fitted likelihood function of the model and Bayesian Information Criterion (BIC) as an estimate of a function of the posterior probability of a model being true under a certain Bayesian setup, so that a lower BIC means that a model is considered to be more likely to be the true model, while a lower AIC means a model is considered to be closer to the truth (Burnham and Anderson 2002, pp. 271–289).

For the baseline model we took Naik and Raman's model (2003, pp. 377–378):

$$S_t = \alpha + \beta_1 u_t + \beta_2 v_t + \lambda S_{t-1} + \kappa_1 u_t v_t + \kappa_2 u_t S_{t-1} + \kappa_3 v_t S_{t-1} + v_t$$

Where S_t is sales at time t, u_t, v_t present an advertising effort at time t for both advertising media (u, v), α represents the mean level of initial sales in the absence of advertising, β is the short-term effect of advertising, λ is the carryover effect of advertising, κ is synergy when combined sales impact of (u, v) exceeds the sum of the independent effects β, parameters (κ2, κ3) represent the moderating effects of current advertising on carryover effect and v_t is a normally distributed error term (Naik and Raman 2003, pp. 378).

We modified the existing model, adding two more communication chan-nels and tracking sales for each channel separately. From a complete model definition (first step of the analysis) the following model was proposed by a stepwise selection procedure selecting the best model based on the least Aikake Information Criterion (AIC) value:

$$S_t = \alpha + \beta_1 t_t + \beta_2 w_t + \lambda_1 S_{t\text{-}2}^t + \lambda_2 S_{t\text{-}2}^i + \lambda_3 S_{t\text{-}2}^r + \lambda_4 S_{t\text{-}2}^w +$$
$$\kappa_1 t_t i_t + \kappa_2 t_t r_t + \kappa_3 t_t w_t + \kappa_4 i_t w_t + \kappa_5 i_t w_t + \kappa_7 t_t S_{t\text{-}2}^w +$$
$$\kappa_8 i_t S_{t\text{-}2}^t + \kappa_9 i_t \nu\ \kappa_{10} w_t S_{t\text{-}2}^t + \kappa_{11} w_t S_{t\text{-}2}^i + \kappa_{12} w_t S_{t\text{-}2}^r +$$
$$\kappa_{13} r_t S_{t\text{-}2}^w + peak + bottom + \nu_t$$

Where S_{t-2}^t, S_{t-2}^i, S_{t-2}^r, S_{t-2}^w denote sales due to television, Internet, retail and wholesale activities, respectively; ($\lambda 1$, $\lambda 2$, $\lambda 3$, $\lambda 4$) are carryover effects of tel-evision, Internet, retail and wholesale channels (t, i, r, w); κ represents both simulations and sequential synergy; that is, the combined sales impact of (t, i, r, w) and the moderating effects of current advertising on the carryover effect. We denote the sum of sales with St, television advertising expressed in minutes with tt, on-line activities expressed in number of visitors per day with it and retail activities in number of shops opened, loyalty scheme programme in the corresponding period in t = 1...207 weeks (4 years). Both dummy vari-ables are used to capture seasonal effects; vt is a normally distributed error term that represents the impact of other factors not included in the model.

3. Results

Previous articles built models that retain all the important parameter that may have an influence on sales in the model at all times. By expanding the model, the number of parameters to be included in the model expands significantly. In order to preserve parsimony we incorporated only the im-portant variables into the model and interactions. We selected the best model based on the least AIC.

Advertising effectiveness is typically measured through econometric mod-els that measure the impact of varying levels of advertising. The effect of communication channels on sales is split into direct and indirect effect. The indirect effect is defined as a direct consequence of advertising on sales. The indirect effect on the other hand is described as synergy between communication channels. It is possible to prove that advertising activities that do not have a direct effect on sales can affect sales through synergy.

For better understanding, we divided our model into four interrelated parts (see Table 1): direct or main effects, carryover effects, simultaneous synergy, sequential synergy and covariates. Influences must be interpreted taking the whole model into consideration.

Table 1: Multiple regression estimates

Model parameters	Estimate	Std. Error	t value
Main effects			
Effectiveness of TV advertising, β1	0.85	0.18	4.80
Effectiveness of Wholesale Loyalty scheme, β2	2.17	0.28	7.63
Carryover effects			
TV carryover effect , λ1	-0.45	0.23	-1.98
Internet carryover effect , λ2	0.31	0.05	6.10
Wholesale carryover effect , λ3	0.64	0.23	2.75
Retail carryover effect , λ4	0.88	0.22	3.94
Simultaneous synergy			
Synergy between TV and Internet, κ1	-0.73	0.15	-4.69
Synergy between TV and Retail shops, κ2	0.18	0.07	2.62
Synergy between TV and Wholesale Loyalty scheme, κ3	0.20	0.23	0.86
Synergy between Internet and Wholesale Loyalty scheme, κ4	-0.28	0.13	-2.17
Synergy between Retail shops and Wholesale Loyalty sch., κ5	-0.51	0.20	-2.58
Sequential synergy			
Synergy between TV and Wholesale carryover effect, κ6	-0.78	0.23	-3.43
Synergy between Internet and Retail carryover effect, κ7	-0.33	0.19	-1.76

Model parameters	Estimate	Std. Error	t value
Synergy between Internet and TV carryover effect, κ8	0.91	0.22	4.07
Synergy between Internet and Wholesale carryover effect, κ9	1.22	0.21	5.78
Synergy between Wholesale Loyalty scheme and TV carryover effect, κ10	-0.59	0.16	-3.78
Synergy between Wholesale Loyalty scheme and Internet carryover effect, κ11	-0.52	0.17	-3.00
Synergy between Wholesale Loyalty scheme and Retail carryover effect, κ12	-0.48	0.12	-3.91
Synergy between Retail no. of shops and Wholesale carryover effect, κ13	-0.72	0.15	-4.72
Covariates			
Dummy peak (binary)	0.11	0.06	1.84
Dummy bottom (binary)	-0.12	0.07	-1.77
AIC BIC	97.59 177.59		

When considering direct effects television advertising and wholesale loyalty programmes have a significant positive influence on the outcome. Among carryover effects, sales through television have a significant negative influence on the outcome, while all other included channels have a significant positive influence on the outcome. When adding channels into the model we can see that relations between existing variables change. When keeping only television and Internet in the model we could notice a positive synergy now turned into negative. Simultaneous synergy between television and the Internet has a significant negative effect on sales. Simultaneous synergies are significant and negative also for synergies between the Internet and wholesale and retail and wholesale. We can then speak of media cannibalization of total sales when the Internet and television work simultaneously – the same consists between the Internet and wholesale and retail and wholesale.

In general, total sales decay in time, with sales related to the company stores an exception. Since people prefer to check the product before buying, company stores with highly motivated employees (personal selling) are becoming the most effective over time. Input in minutes on air is declining every year; visits to web pages are quite stable, even slowly rising. Sequential synergies also have a significant effect on sales. Synergy between minutes on air (television) and wholesale carry over effect represent a negative moderating effect of current advertising on carryover effect; so we can determine that the current advertising decline relates to the carryover effect (Naik and Raman 2003, pp. 376–380). Negative significant synergy occurs between wholesale and television, the Internet and the retail carry over effect, as well as between the number of own shops and the wholesale carryover effect.

It must be taken into consideration that television advertising decreases or increases depending on the decline or increase of sales (budgets are dependent on sales level/results).

4. Discussion and conclusion

The impact of communication channels on sales is both direct and indirect. Direct impact is a result of the effectiveness of communication channels, while indirect impact is visible through the phenomenon of synergy. According to Raman and Naik (2006, pp. 491), we define synergy as an increase in the effectiveness of each marketing communication channel due to the presence of other channels.

By incorporating variables measuring advertising effectiveness in the econometric model we could measure the impact of each communication channel and synergy. From our previous work we know that when synergy is present, an increase in optimal advertising budget is encouraged and the optimal spending level rises. However, the budget must be spent in such a way that it is most likely to create stronger synergistic effects across media (Suklan and Žabkar 2013, pp. 162). At this point we encounter negative synergy, meaning negative effects if cross-media consumption results in the sum being less than the individual parts. This could occur through distraction in the process of multitasking or though media cannibalization, in which exposure to one medium occurs at the expense of another (Assael 2011, pp. 7).

Marketers are aware of correlations between actions and sales. Throughout the selling process they are in search of important triggers that influence the audience toward the purchasing of products as well as analysing other important elements that have an important impact on sales. Often it seems that advertising has no direct impact on sales, but creates awareness and acts as a reminder of the intent to purchase. The actual purchase depends mainly on the price, promotions, and product quality and distribution channels.

To summarize, we developed a marketing-mix model that provides insights into how input and output components of the model interact. The dependent variable is measured in actual value of total units sold. To some extent brand awareness is incorporated in the model through carryover effects of the independent variables. Four communication channels were integrated into the model (television, on-line, own shops/retail, wholesale), which allowed us to foresee the roles of each component included in the model and its impact on sales. Through the analysis we contribute to understanding consumer responses to cross-media strategies.

List of references

Assael, Henry: "From Silos to Synergy. A Fifty-year Review of Cross-media Research Shows Synergy Has Yet to Achieve its Full Potential". *Journal of Advertising Research* 51(1), 2011, pp. 42–58.

Burnham, Kenneth P. / Anderson, David R.: "Model selection and multi-model inference: a practical information-theoretic approach". Springer: 2002.

Coughlan, Anne T. /Choi, Chan S. / Chu, Wujin / Ingene, Charles A. / Moorthy, Sridhar / Padmanabhan, V. / Raju, Jagmohan, S. / Soberman, David A. /Staelin, Richard/ Zhang, John Z.: "Marketing modeling reality and the realities of marketing modelling". *Marketing Letters*, 21(3), 2010, pp. 317–333.

Enoch, Glenn/Johnson, Kelly: "Cracking the Cross-Media Code. How to Use Single-Source Measures to Examine Media Cannibalization and Convergence". *Journal of Advertising Research* 50(2), 2010, pp. 125–136.

Havlena, William/ Cardarelli, Robert /de Montigny, Michelle: "Quantifying the isolated and synergistic effects of exposure frequency for TV, print, and Internet advertising". *Journal of Advertising Research* 47(3), 2007, pp. 215–221.

Kabacoff, Robert: "R in Action". Manning Publications Co: 2011.

Keller, Kevin Lane: "Brand equity management in a multichannel, multimedia retail environment". *Journal of Interactive Marketing* 24(2), 2010, pp. 58–70.

Kollmann, Tobias / Kuckertz, Andreas / Kayser, Ina: "Cannibalization or synergy? Consumers' channel selection in online–offline multichannel systems". *Journal of Retailing and Consumer Services* 19(2), 2012, pp. 186–194.

Naik, Prasad A. / Peters, Kay: "A Hierarchical Marketing Communications Model of Online and Offline Media Synergies". *Journal of Interactive Marketing* 23(4), 2009, pp. 288–299.

Naik, Prasad A. / Raman, Kalyan / Winer, Russell S: "Planning marketing-mix strategies in the presence of interaction effects". *Marketing Science* 24(1), 2005, pp. 25–34.

Naik, Prasad A. / Raman, Kalyan: "Understanding the impact of synergy in multimedia communications". *Journal of Marketing Research*, 40(4), 2003, pp. 375–388.

Prasad, Ashutosh /Sethi, Suresh P: "Integrated marketing communications in markets with uncertainty and competition". *Automatica* 45(3), 2009, pp. 601–610.

Raman, Kalyan / Naik, Prasad A.: "Integrated Marketing Communications in Retailing". *Retailing in the 21st Century* 2006, pp. 381–395.

Suklan, Jana / Žabkar, Vesna: "Modeling Synergies in Cross-Media Strategies: On-line and Off-line Media". Advances in Advertising Research (Vol. IV). Springer: 2013, pp. 159–171.

Weisberg, Sanford / Fox, John: "An R companion to applied regression". Sage Publications, Incorporated: 2010.

Boštjan Delak
ITAD, Revizija in svetovanje, d.o.o. Technology Park Ljubljana
Pot za Brdom 100, 1000 Ljubljana, Slovenia, www.itad.si
bostjan.delak@itad.si

How to identify knowledge and evaluate knowledge management in organization through information system analysis

Abstract: Knowledge is recognized as the most important strategic asset every organization has. It is very important to identify, capture/acquire, share, reuse and unlearn knowledge. These activities are managed through Knowledge Management [KM]. It is a rather challenging task to evaluate the level of KM in an organization. The paper presents two approaches, COBIT5 and Framework for Information System Due Diligence [FISDD], to be used for knowledge and KM level identification. The research objective is to identify which approach could identify KM levels in the organization more quickly and effectively. The research evaluation is based on two real case studies, where both approaches have been used. The analysis had four phases, which are described. The results identify that both approaches could be used. There are some pros and cons of the approaches. Some ideas for future work are presented.

Keywords: Knowledge, Knowledge management, COBIT5, Framework for Information System Due Diligence, Information System Analysis

1. Introduction

The next step beyond data and information is knowledge (Gray 1999). Knowledge is recognized as the most important strategic asset that each organization has. Knowledge is epistemologically classified in two dimensions: tacit and explicit, and from an organization's perspective, has two distinct goals: generate knowledge and apply knowledge (Chou 2005). It is very important to identify, capture/acquire, share, reuse and unlearn knowledge. This is managed through knowledge management [KM]. Moos et al. argued that a key challenge is to disclose how an organization can acquire and utilize relevant knowledge (Moos et al. 2011) and how this is related to an organization's innovative success. Nonaka (1991, p. 96) described that "*in an economy where the only certainty is uncertainty, the one sure source of lasting competitive advantage is knowledge*" and he also explained how Japanese organizations are dealing with knowledge, innovations and their success. Nonaka & Konno described how Japanese organizations are managing the place [*"ba"*] to locate the knowledge and how to share it (Nonaka / Konno 1998, p. 41). A further issue is knowledge sharing. There are several research papers describing this topic. Pirhonen & Vartiainen (2007, p. 7) argued, which kind of knowledge transfer is required to reduce the risks when replacing a project manager. Nodari et al. made a review of scientific writings and a research model that relates the intra-organizational and inter-organizational sharing process of absorptive capacity and organizational performance (Nodari / Oliveira / Maçada 2013). Recently, numerous scientific papers describing knowledge creation in software development teams have been published. Spohrer et al. (2013) described the role of pair programming and peer code review. Dissanayake et al. described knowledge creation in agile software development and the important aspect of creativity (Dissanayake / Dantu / Nerur 2013).

A great challenge is how to identify the level of: knowledge, knowledge identification, knowledge creation, KM and knowledge sharing in the observed organization. Henczel suggested performing an information audit as the first step towards KM evaluation (Henczel 2000, p. 211). The author is trying to find an answer to her question whether an information system [IS] audit or IS analysis could define the level of KM in the observed organization and the plan how to get this result is described further in this paper. The need to measure knowledge resources within the organization has therefore emerged as a key area of interest for both researchers and practitioners within the knowledge management domain (Rosemann / Chan 2000, p. 1341).

The paper is organized as follows. In the next section the term knowledge, knowledge life cycle, KM and KM systems are presented through a literature review. This is followed by a brief presentation of two approaches for IS analysis – COBIT5 and Framework for Information System Due Diligence [FISDD] as a methodology used in the research. Section four describes the motivation behind the research, which is followed by a description of the research. The case studies with the results are presented in section five. Discussion describes the results and related work. Finally, the conclusion outlines the implications of the research in practice and further possible research activities.

2. Literature Review

Knowledge is considered to be an important resource to maintain the competitiveness of an organization (Mahapatra / Sarkar 2000, p. 1288). Nonaka & Takeuchi have defined knowledge by comparing it with information – *"Knowledge, unlike information is about beliefs and commitment"* (Nonaka / Takeuchi, 1995, p. 58). They say knowledge, *"like information, is about meaning"*. Ragab & Arisha stated that, *"Knowledge is the currency of the current economy, a vital organizational asset and a key to creating a sustainable competitive advantage"* (Ragab /Arisha 2013, p. 873). One of the simplest definitions of knowledge management is: *"conscious strategy of getting the right knowledge to the right people at the right time and helping people share and put information into action in ways that strive to improve organizational performance"* (O'dell / Grayson 1998, p. 6).

Knowledge is an asset, but its value is much harder to assess than that of physical assets. Knowledge may be categorized into two types: tacit and explicit (Nonaka / Takeuchi, 1995). Polanyi defines tacit knowledge as personal, context-specific and thus not easily visible and expressible – nor easy to formalize and communicate to others (Polanyi 1966). Professor Levy described tacit knowledge very graphically, *"what someone has between the ears"*. On the other hand, Polanyi refers to explicit knowledge as being transmittable in some systematic language – such words, numbers, diagrams or models (Polanyi 1966). Nonaka & Takeuchi expand Polanyi's tacit knowledge into two dimensions, technical and cognitive. Technical is often referred to as "know-how" and the other consists of beliefs, ideals, values, schemata and mental models (Nonaka / Takeuchi, 1995). Knowledge creation takes place through the transformation of tacit knowledge to explicit and back as Nonaka and Takeuchi explained in their knowledge life cycle with a knowledge spiral that contains the following phases: socialization, externalization, combination and internalization (Nonaka / Takeuchi, 1995).

Over the past few years, papers have described further developments of KM. Some of them described the different approaches from knowledge to

KM, e.g. from tacit knowledge to KM (Kakabadse / Kouzmin 2001). KM is *"an effort to increase useful knowledge in the organization"* as explained by McInerney (McInerney 2002, p. 1014), adding that *"KM promotes the sharing of appropriate knowledge artifacts"*. As nowadays ICT plays an important role in major competitive organizations, several papers refer to the role of ICT in KM (Mahapatra / Sarkar 2000). Rosemann & Chan define the framework for enterprise knowledge. They identify stages of the knowledge life cycle: identification, creation, transfer, storage, reuse and unlearning of knowledge (Rosemann / Chan 2000, p. 1336).

Chen & Edington argued that measurement of knowledge is one of the most difficult KM activities (Chen / Edington 2005, p. 306). The need to measure the knowledge within an organization emerged as a key area of interest for both researchers and practitioners within a KM domain. There are different frameworks and methodologies to measure the knowledge: for instance MinK [Measuring Individual Knowledge] as presented by Arisha & Ragab (Arisha / Ragab 2013). Tow et al. (2011) argued about very first activity within each organization – knowledge identification, and it is most important on how an organization manages the flow of knowledge (Tow / Venable / Dell 2011). Kankanhalli and Tan presented several approaches for measuring the KM which includes: House of Quality [QFD – Quality Function Deployment], Balanced Scorecard and American Productivity Center [APQC], Skandia Navigator, IC index and Intangible Assets Monitor (Kankanhalli / Tan 2005). Smith & McKeen presented several frameworks for KM evaluation, they argued the importance of: paying attention to what is measured; no silver bullet; importance of business metrics; measurement of different levels; monitor leading indicators and clarify what value means (Smith / McKeen 2005).

In the presence there are and in the future there will be scholars and practitioners with their researches on knowledge and KM related frameworks.

3. Methodologies

There are several methods, standards, tools, and frameworks that can be used to conduct, analyze, or deliver a specific type of IS analysis and IS due diligence on a particular IS area/domain.

3.1 COBIT5 Framework

The COBIT framework is seen as the de facto standard of Information Technology [IT] Governance (Burtscher / Manwani / Remenyi 2009), and its background is as follows. In 1977, the Electronic Data Processing Auditors Association [EDPAA] issued a set of issues and guidelines for IT audit and control, which were the predecessor of COBIT. In 1994, EDPAA changed its name to ISACA [Information System Audit and Control Association] (Guldentops 2011), and in 1996, issued COBIT for use in IT audit. Over the years, the scope of COBIT was extended as follows: IT control – COBIT2 [1998]; IT management – COBIT3 [2000]; IT governance – COBIT4 [2005], Enterprise IT Governance – COBIT5 [2012] – last updated framework, which included as a goal: "Knowledge, expertise and initiatives for business innovation" (ISACA 2012, p. 19).

COBIT5 provides the next generation of ISACA's guidance on the enterprise and management of IT. This version is aligned with other IS frameworks and IS best practices such as: Information Technology Infrastructure Library [ITIL], The Open Group Architecture Forum [TOGAF], Project Management Body of Knowledge [PMBOK], Projects in Controlled Environments 2 [PRINCE2], and International Organization for Standardization [ISO] standards (ISACA 2012). COBIT5 framework also enlarges the different positions and roles regarding responsibilities for implementing processes.

The COBIT5 framework makes a clear distinction between governance and management. There are five processes related to governance and 32 processes related to the management of enterprise IT. Within these processes, two directly cover knowledge, knowledge management and knowledge sharing: APO07– Manage human resources. The process description for APO07 is: "*Provide a structured approach to ensure optimal structuring, placement, decision rights and skills of human resources. This includes communicating the defined roles and responsibilities, learning and growth plans, and performance expectations, supported by competent and motivated people*" (ISACA 2013a, p. 121); and its purpose to "*optimize human resource capabilities to meet enterprise objectives*". The process description for BAI08 is to "*Maintain the availability of relevant, current, validated and reliable knowledge to support all process activities and to facilitate decision making. Plan for the identification, gathering, organizing, main-taining, use and retirement of knowledge"* (ISACA 2012, p. 129) and its purpose is: *"provide the knowledge required to support all staff in their work activities and for informed decision making and enhanced produc-tivity"*. The COBIT5 framework also enlarges the different positions and roles regarding responsibilities for implementing processes. IS auditors all over the globe, members of ISACA, use the COBIT5 framework in their day-to-day operations.

3.2 Framework for Information System Due Diligence

The IS field lacks a scientifically based analytical tool for rapid delivery of IS due diligence. Bhatia explained how important it is to follow a structured method for the due diligence activities (Bhatia 2007, p. 49). In the world there are no standard guidelines for the implementation of IS due diligence activities. There are quite a few approaches, standards, methodologies and best practices to perform these tasks. Delak and Bajec (2013b) indicated possible ways of implementation due to diligence. On the other hand, there have been various analyses of IS implementation carried out . There are several types of IS due to diligence: Initial, General, Vendor, and Technology. Briefly: Initial IS due diligence should be conducted prior to the merger or acquisition of any organization. IS due diligence may be referred to as general, when it is used upon the request of shareholders or an organization's top management to get the status of an important part of IS or complete status of IS within the organization (Spendding 2005, p. 123). When an organization decides to outsource some or even all its IS processing activities, vendor IS due diligence (Bayuk 2009) should be performed prior to the actual IS outsourcing. Technology due diligence (Andriole 2007) is performed on prospective technology investments.

The FISDD enables delivery of a rapid IS due diligence and also has an integrated decision model. This framework consists of four phases: preparation, realization / on-site review, analysis, and decision. Each of these phases involve specific activities, sub-processes, supporting documents [questionnaires, templates, etc.], and results. The time frame for each phase may vary depending on the size of the observed organization, the location[s] and available documentation. Other vital parts of the framework include predefined questionnaires, different types of reports and the decision model (Delak / Bajec 2013b). The FISDD approach with some basic questions regarding KM was earlier used in some cases to identify KM in IS due diligence processes (Delak / Bajec 2013a).

4. Motivations

As knowledge is important, assets as well as author frequently make different IS analysis [e.g. IS due diligences, IS audits] his motivation was to identify, which approach is the most suitable for identifying knowledge in the observed organization. The researchers' motivation was to expand some FISDD' questionnaires for KM evaluation and test it in the real case studies. Given that ISACA announced upgraded COBIT framework, it may be sensible to test COBIT5's two processes as the tool for KM evaluation as well.

The hypotheses are:

H1: With COBIT5 you can identify explicit knowledge and also some tacit knowledge in the observed organization and its ICT.
H2: With FISDD you can identify explicit knowledge and also some tactic knowledge in the observed organization and its ICT.

Both hypotheses have been transferred into the following research questions:

Q1: Is it possible to identify explicit knowledge and also tacit knowledge in the observed organization and its ICT with FISDD?
Q2: Is it possible to assess the level of KM in the observed organization with COBIT5 framework?

Both hypotheses have been evaluated through real case studies and field studies through interviews with two different organizations in different industries. Based on the results, there might be some activities for possible upgrades of both approaches.

5. Proposed research

Two real case studies have been conducted with both approaches to get answers to the above mentioned hypothesizes. The proposed research consists of four phases: phase one – upgrade of FISDD framework with KM related questions; phase two – define IS audit program for KM identification with

COBIT5 methodology; phase three – select organizations for case studies; and phase four – perform case studies.

The last phase had three sub-goals: establish the status of KM system in the observed organization and how knowledge creation is documented, and identify explicit and tacit knowledge in the ICT team.

Researchers have prepared special subset of FISDD main questionnaire [IS status questionnaire] based on Delak & Bajec (2013b), to synthesize important sub-questions, which are relevant for knowledge and KM. This "IS status KM questionnaire" has 8 domains: General; Audit; IS management; IS resources; Information Security; Application – development, procurement, implementation and maintenance; Business Continue Management; and Business processes reengineering and risk management; with 179 questions. Researchers have conducted an open interview when filling in FISDD IS status KM questionnaire.

For COBIT5 framework, researchers selected two COBIT5's processes – Manage human resources [APO07] and Manage knowledge [BAI08] (ISACA 2012). Researchers have prepared COBIT5 KM questionnaire, based on the activities described within the document – *COBIT5 Enabling processes*. These activities of each process described how to implement process and their management practices with predefined activities in a total of fifty different questions. Researchers have conducted closed interview when fulfilling the COBIT5 KM questionnaire, where possible answers were: yes, no, partially. The full content of the both questionnaires can be disclosed upon request made to the author.

5.1 Case Studies Results

The case studies were delivered at the end of 2013 in two companies in Slovenia, one is an internationally oriented software development company with its products installed in most continents of the globe [further on: Company INT], and the other one is a small IS consultancy and IS audit company dealing with national customers [further on: Company NAT]. The approach was the same for both companies; with both CEOs researchers have had two interviews. For FISDD framework, the interview took three hours, comparable to COBIT5 framework, which took one hour. The time difference was where the FISDD framework has open interviews, while for

COBIT5 KM questionnaire had closed interviews, [with possible answers], where researchers were looking for the existence of defined activities with possible options [for answer]: yes, partially and no. Analyses were completed at the beginning of December 2013 and took half a day each. The results are in a form of a subjective evaluation, performed by the analyser. To evaluate the answers, and to compare the companies, researchers have converted their answers to numeric values. During the next step, a numeric transformation for COBIT5 km questionnaire has been done: yes – 2 points; partially – 1 point; and no – 0 point. Sub questions have been added and divided by the number of sub questions, the result was the value of specific question / management practice activities. Table 1 presents the results for COBIT5 framework for selected two processes – Manage Human resources and Knowledge management for both companies.

Table 1: Results of COBIT5 KM questionnaire

	COBIT5 Knowledge Management Questionnaire	Company INT	Company NAT
ID	Management practices \ total score	**1.34**	**0.71**
APO07 Manage Human Resources		**1.55**	**0.84**
APO07.01	Maintain adequate and appropriate staffing	2.00	1.20
APO07.02	Identify key IT personnel.	1.25	1.00
APO07.03	Maintain the skills and competencies of personnel	1.29	0.71
APO07.04	Evaluate employee job performance	1.50	0.63
APO07.05	Plan and track the usage of IT and business human resources	1.75	0.75
APO07.06	Manage contract staff	1.50	0.75
BAI08 Manage Knowledge		**1.10**	**0.55**
BAI08.01	Nurture and facilitate a knowledge-sharing culture	2.00	0.60
BAI08.02	Identify and classify sources of information	0.75	0.75

	COBIT5 Knowledge Management Questionnaire	Company INT	Company NAT
BAI08.03	Organise and contextualise information into knowledge	1.25	0.75
BAI08.04	Use and share knowledge.	1.00	0.67
BAI08.05	Evaluate and retire information.	0.50	0.00

Table 1 presents the calculated results for COBIT5 KM questionnaire for both companies. Our research shows that Company INT has partially implemented both processes [total score is 1,34], where the COBIT5 score for Manage Human Resources is 1,55 and the score for Manage Knowledge is 1,10. For Company NAT, our research also indicates some implementation of the implemented knowledge management process [total score is 0,71], which correlated with their COBIT5 score, which was almost half of the Company INT.

The FISDD framework KM questionnaire has also been converted to numerical figures. The textual answers have been converted to next numeric values: 1, 0.75, 0.5, 0.25 and 0. Researchers on subjective evaluations have done the conversion. The results are presented in table 2.

Table 2 presents the calculated results for the FISDD KM questionnaire for both companies. Our research shows that company INT has higher marks than company NAT. The results can be compared with ISO/IEC 15504 capability process levels [0 – Incomplete, 1 – Performed, 2 – Managed, 3 – Established, 4 – Predictable, 5 – Optimizing]. Based on such a scale from 0 to 1, Company INT – could be evaluated or marked as level 2 – Managed process, where on the other hand Company NAT is evaluated with level 1 – Performed process.

Table 2: Results of FISDD KM questionnaire

Questionnaire Chapter's Description	Company INT	Company NAT
Initial data	0.8000	0.7000
Audit documentation	0.2500	0.0000
Governance	0.6018	0.2973

Questionnaire Chapter's Description	Company INT	Company NAT
Resources	0.3750	0.1615
Security / Protection	0.5313	0.4219
Business Continuity Management	0.1016	0.0313
Development and maintenance	0.6094	0.2135
Business Process Evaluation and Risk Management	0.2000	0.0750
Average	0.4336	0.2376

To validate our approach, management of both companies also completed a self-assessment questionnaire provided by ISACA (2013b). Results from company INT shown that the company is at 3rd process capability level – "Managed" from 6 possible capability levels for both reviewed processes, which correlated with the result from COBIT5, that is: "PA 2.1 Performance Management" (ISACA 2013b, p. 10). Results from company NAT have shown that the company is at its 2nd process capability level – "Performed", from 6 possible capability levels for both reviewed processes, which is in line with their result from COBIT5 of "PA 1.1 Process Performance" (ISACA 2013b, p. 10).

The pros and cons of both frameworks are presented and explained in the Discussion section. Further work and planned extensions of the case studies are presented in the Conclusion section.

6. Discussion

Our explanatory study has outlined several issues and has answered to both of the research questions. Hypothesis H1: With FISDD you can identify explicit knowledge and also tacit knowledge in the observed organization and its ICT activities, was correct. With FISDD IS status KM questionnaire, you are able to identify explicit knowledge within the organization Analysis from FISDD shown that the score for Company INT is at 3rd level, when the score for Company NAT is at 2nd level. These scores could be transformed also to the knowledge management level. With FISDD you are able to identify some basic information about Intellectual Capital [IC] within observed organization. This information could not be compared with different IC evaluations. Costa & Ramos (2014) evaluate even further and evaluate IC based on Analytic Hierarchy Process. Skyrme mentioned that, "If you're not keeping score, you're only practicing" (Skyrme 2003, p. 3). He continues that in order to keep score you need to develop a measurement system using measures, appropriate to each business unit. Stewart (1998) describes meaningful measurements for intellectual capital, which can be divided into three categories: human capital, structural capital and relationship capital. None of the defined categories are integrated in FISDD framework or to COBIT5.

H2: With COBIT5 you can assess the level of KM in the observed organization and its ICT, was correct. Table 2 has shown the case study results. Research analysis has shown that with this framework, it is not possible to evaluate level of knowledge, either tacit or explicit and it is not possible to evaluate intellectual capital [associated with employees] within the organization. COBIT5 does not integrate any widely used human capital methods such as Human capital readiness, Human capital index and human capital monitor, which was presented in the critical review of knowledge and knowledge management done by Ragab & Arisha (2013). ISACA, with the COBIT5 framework defines for each process stakeholder [either external or internal], with his or her own roles and associated responsibility levels, a RACI matrix – who is responsible, accountable, consulted and informed for each process (ISACA 2012). According to the ISACA definition for process Manage human resources chief information officer is accountable for all management practices. Process Manage knowledge is more complicated and role of accountability for this management practice is divided into different positions – business executives, chief information officer and business process owners (ISACA 2012). ISACA within COBIT5 does not appoint a chief knowledge officer [CKO] to lead company's knowledge efforts, which is a lack of responsibility appointments, as this role might be one of the important responsibility roles in the future. Harlow (2014) argues that currently only a few empirical studies exist, which detail the relationships of knowledge management executives such as CKO and chief learning officers.

Although COBIT5 has abovementioned cons, it also has some pros, with these processes and usage of COBIT5 enabling processes management practice activities you are able to very effectively evaluate the level of KM.

On the other hand FISDD is more oriented to knowledge identification. ISACA with Enabling Process are not in the position to measure the process, the same is with FISDD framework where KM level is subjective definition. Another dimension of influence of organization performance – trust is not supported in FISDD or in COBIT5 framework.

In general the COBIT5 KM questionnaire could be better and quicker used for KM evaluation within the observed company. On the other hand FISDD KM questionnaire could be better used for knowledge evaluation within the observed company.

The contribution of this paper is to inform scholars, researchers and others interested about the vast possibilities to use FISDD and COBIT5 frameworks in order to identify knowledge and the level of knowledge management in an organization.

6.1 Limitation

There are several limitations. Primarily, the number of case studies is low, it was very first check for both frameworks to be evaluated in practice for knowledge management brief evaluation. Second the research sample based on a small number of companies in one country – Slovenia. Third the paper does not analyse and compare used frameworks with other knowledge management maturity models [KMMM] and assessments such as KMMM capstone project undertaken by Kent State University (Bedford et al. 2014) or KMMM presented by Ehms & Langen (2002). There are several areas which have not been captured by this research, e.g. Aggestam et al. identified a specific type of risk – knowledge loss (Aggestam / Söderström /Persson 2010). They identified seven types of knowledge loss; or knowledge management and project management described by Handzic & Durmic (2014) or even the knowledge sharing, which are nicely explained by Hendricks: *"The key to success in knowledge sharing is that the personal ambition should match the group ambition. Therefore, also the touchstone for successful ICT applications for knowledge sharing is the question how they relate to these ambitions, and to the motivation of knowledge workers to match them. (Hendriks 1999, p. 94)"*

7. Conclusion

Farhadi argued how important knowledge management [KM] audit due diligence is, with the aim of explaining the relationship between intangible knowledge [tacit knowledge], assets and inorganic business growth through mergers and acquisitions (Farhadi 2009). He added a new dimension to the area of due diligence in general, as well as special IS due diligences. Jennex & Olfman (2005) described four different KMS success modules and presented a framework for assessing KMS success. Such an approach is valid for organizations with implementing KMS, which might not be suitable for due diligence activities. Paliszkiewich & Koohang (2013) done the research on how organizational trust has a positive influence on organizational performance. They mention that modern organizations have identified the importance of trust related to KM as a mean to gain and sustain competitive advantage. She states that trust among employees is an essential prerequisite for knowledge sharing. Trust is more a social competence and this kind of evaluation would require additional questionnaires and additional resources, so researchers decided not to include it in this research.

The contribution of this paper is that both described frameworks could be used for brief knowledge management evaluation, especially if there is a time limitation of such an activity. Both frameworks are daily used for different objectives as knowledge and knowledge management evaluation. The paper also presents pros and cons of both frameworks for such an evaluation.

The author's future work includes some additional analysis of the FISDD areas related to KM and KM level evaluation and possible cooperation with ISACA in order to upgrade COBIT5 with additional KM activities.

Bibliography

Aggestam, Lena / Söderström, Eva / Persson, Anne: "Seven Types of Knowledge Loss in the Knowledge Capture Process". *Proceedings of European Conference on Information Systems (ECIS2010)*, 2010. Paper 13.

Andriole, Stephen J.: "Mining for Digital Gold: Technology Due Diligence for CIOs". *Communications of the Association for Information Systems*, 2007, (20:24), pp. 371–381.

Arisha, Amr / Ragab, Mohamed: "The MinK Framework: Developing Metrics for the Measurement of Individual Knowledge". *Proceeding of Knowledge & Information Management Conference (KIM2013), UK.* 2013.

Bayuk, Jennifer L.: "Vendor Due Diligence". *ISACA Journal*, 2009, (3), pp. 34–38.

Bedford, Denise A. D. / Camp, Margaret / Hein, Dessie / Liston, Tyler / Oxendine, Jeffery / Testa, Dean: "Developing an Open Source Adaptable and Sustainable Method for Conducting Knowledge Management Maturity Modeling and Assessment". *Proceedings of European Conference on knowledge Management*, 2014, Vol. 1, pp. 111–119.

Bhatia, Mohan: "IT Merger Due Diligence – A Blueprint". *Information System Control Journal*, 2007, (1), pp. 46–49.

Burtscher, Christoph / Manwani Sharm / Remenyi, Dan: "Towards A Conceptual Map Of IT Governance: A Review Of Current Academic And Practitioner Thinking". *UK Academy for Information Systems Conference Proceedings 2009*, 2009, Paper 15.

Chen, Andrew N.K. / Edington, Theresa M.: "Assessing Value in Organizational Knowledge Creation: Considerations for Knowledge Workers". *MIS Quarterly*, 2005, 29 (2), pp. 279–309.

Chou, Shih-Wei: "Knowledge creation: absorptive capacity, organizational mechanisms, and knowledge storage/retrieval capabilities". *Journal of Information Science*, 2005, 31 (6), pp. 453–465.

Costa, Ricardo / Ramos, Ana Paula: "Designing and Testing an AHP Methodology to Prioritize Critical Intellectual Capital Elements for Product Innovation". *Proceedings of European Conference on knowledge Management*, 2014, Vol. 1, pp. 223–232.

Delak, Boštjan / Bajec, Marko: "Information system due diligence data as an input for knowledge management". *Online journal of applied knowledge management*, 2013, 1 (2), pp. 15–24.

Delak, Boštjan / Bajec, Marko: "Framework for the delivery of information system due diligence". *Information systems management*. 2013, 30 (1), pp. 137–149.

Dissanayake, Indika / Dantu, Ramakrishna / Nerur, Sridhar: "Knowledge Management in Software Development: The Case of Agile Software". *Proceedings of Americas Conference on Information Systems (AMCIS 2013)*, 2013.

Ehms Karsten / Langen Manfred: "Holistic Development of Knowledge Management with KMMM", *Siemens AG Corporate Technology*, 2002

Farhadi, Mehdi: "Intellectual Assets & Knowledge Due Diligence". University of Reading – Henley Business School, UK. 2009. retrieved 1.2.2014, from http://ssrn.com/abstract=1359663.

Gray, Paul: "Knowledge management". *Proceedings of the Americans Conference on Information Systems (AMCIS1999)*, 1999, Paper 292.

Guldentops, Erik: "Where Have All the Control Objectives Gone? They Have Picked Them Every One". *ISACA Journal*, 2011, 4, pp. 6–9.

Handzic, Meliha / Durmic, Nermina: "Merging Knowledge Management with Project Management". *Proceedings of European Conference on knowledge Management*, 2014, Vol. 1, pp. 402–409.

Harlow, Harold: "An Empirical Comparison Study of the Effect of Chief Knowledge Management Officers and Knowledge Management Systems on Innovation and Financial Outcomes". *Proceedings of European Conference on knowledge Management*. 2014, Vol. 1, pp. 410–418.

Harold, Rebecca: *Managing an Information Security and Privacy Awareness and Training Program*. 2nd., CRC Press, Taylor and Francis Group, Boca Raton, FL, USA, 2011, pp. 10.

Henczel, Susan: "The information audit as a first step towards effective Knowledge Management: an opportunity for special librarian". *INSPEL* 34 (3/4), 2000, pp. 210–226.

Hendriks Paul: "Why Share Knowledge? The Influence of ICT on the Motivation for Knowledge Sharing". *Knowledge & Process Management*, 1999, Vol 6, N. 2, pp. 91–100.

ISACA: *COBIT5 Process Enabling*. ISACA, Rolling Meadows, USA, 2012.

ISACA: *COBIT5 for Assurance*. ISACA, Rolling Meadows, USA, 2013.

ISACA: *COBIT Self-assessment Guide: Using COBIT5*. ISACA, Rolling Meadows, USA, 2013.

Jennex, Murray E. / Olfman, Lorne: "Assessing Knowledge Management Success / Effectiveness Models". *International Journal of Knowledge Management (IJKM)*, 2005, 1 (2), pp. 33–49.

Kakabadse, Nada K. / Kouzmin, Alexander / Kakabadse, Andrew: "From Tacit Knowledge to Knowledge Management: Leveraging Invisible Assets". *Knowledge and Process Management*, 2001, 8(3), pp. 137–154.

Kankanhalli, Atreyi / Tan, B.C.Y: "Knowledge Management Metrics: A Review and Directions for Future Research". *International Journal of Knowledge Management*, 2005, 1 (2), pp. 20–32.

Mahapatra, Radha K. / Sarkar, Sumit: "The Role of Information Technology in Knowledge Management". *Proceedings of Americas Conference on Information Systems* (AMCIS2000), 2000, Paper 421.

McInerney, Claire: "Knowledge management and the dynamic nature of knowledge". *Journal of the American Society for Information Science and Technology*. 2002, 53 (12), pp. 1008–1016.

Moos, Bernhard / Beimborn, Daniel / Wagner, Heinz-Theo / Weitzel, Tim: "Knowledge Management Systems, Absorptive Capacity, and Innovation Success". *Proceedings of European Conference on Information Systems (ECIS2011)*, 2011, Paper 145.

Nodari, Felipe / Oliveira, Mirian / Maçada, Antonio Carlos Gastaud: "Knowledge Sharing, Absortive Capacity And Organizational Performance". *Proceedings of European Conference on Information Systems* (ECIS2013), 2013, Paper 69.

Nonaka, Ikujiro: "The Knowledge-Creation Company". *Harvard Business Review*, 1991, pp. 96–104.

Nonaka, Ikujiro / Konno, Noboru: "The Concept of "Ba": Building a Foundation for Knowledge Creation". *California Management Review*, 1998, 40 (3), pp. 40–54.

Nonaka, Ikujiro / Takeuchi, Hirotaka: *The Knowledge-Creating Company*. Oxford University Press. UK. 1995.

O'dell, Carla / Grayson, Jackson C.: *If only we knew what we know: The transfer of internal knowledge and best practice*. Free Press, NY, USA, 1998.

Paliszkiewicz, Joanna / Koohang, Alex: "Organizational trust as a foundation for knowledge sharing and its influence on organizational performance". *Online journal of applied knowledge management*, 2013, 1 (2), pp. 116–127.

Pirhonen, Maritta / Vartiainen, Tero: "Replacing the Project Manager in Information System Projects: What Knowledge Should be Transferred?". *Proceedings of Americas Conference on Information Systems (AMCIS2007)*, 2007, Paper 47.

Polanyi, Michael. *The Tacit Dimension*. The University of Chicago Press, Ltd., London, UK, 1966.

Ragab, Mohamed A.F. / Arisha, Amr: "Knowledge management and measurement: a critical review". *Journal of Knowledge Management*, 2013, 17 (6), pp. 873–901.

Rosemann, Michael / Chan, Roy: "A Framework to Structure Knowledge for Enterprise Systems". *Proceedings of Americas Conference on Information Systems (AMCIS2000)*, 2000, Paper 23.

Skyrme, David J.: *Measuring Knowledge and Intellectual Capital*. Business Intelligence. 2003

Smith, Heather A. / McKeen, James D.: "Developments in Practice XVII: A Framework for KM Evaluation". *Communications of the Associations for Information System*, 2005, Article 9, retrieved 1.2.2014, from http://aisel.aisnet.org/cais/vol16/iss1/9.

Spedding, Linda S.: *Due Diligence and Corporate Governance*, LexisNexis, Antony Rowe, Ltd. Chippenham, Wiltshire, UK, 2004.

Spohrer, Kai / Kude, Thomas / Schmidt, Christoph T. / Heinzl, Armin: "Knowledge Creation In Information Systems Development Teams: The Role Of Pair Programming And Peer Code Review". *Proceedings of European Conference on Information Systems (ECIS2013)*, 2013, Paper 244.

Stewart, Thomas A.: Intellectual Capital: The New Wealth of Organizations, Doubleday, A division of Bantam Doubleday Dell Publishing Group, Inc. New York, NY, USA, 1998.

Tow, William Newk-Fon Hey / Venable, John / Dell, Peter: "Toward More Effective Knowledge Management: An Investigation of Problems in Knowledge Identification". *Proceedings of Pacific Asia Conference on Information Systems (PACIS2011)*, 2011, Paper 194. retrieved 1.2.2014, from http://aisel.aisnet.org/pacis2011/194.

Edo Ravnikar, Borut Lužar, Martin Ravnikar, Roman Šoper
Ambient d.o.o., Mestni trg 25, 1000 Ljubljana, Slovenia
borut.luzar@gmail.com, martin.ravnikar@ambient.si, roman.soper@ambient.si

The Way to Efficient Management of Complex Engineering Design

Abstract: The increasing growth in complexity of architectural and urban design is becoming one of the central issues concerning Architectural, Engineering and Construction (AEC) domains. Current software deliveries, however, are unsuited for dealing with the huge amount of information transacted in the course of the design process. This may primarily be attributed to deficient CAD methodology that underlies the building information modelling initiatives, aimed at efficacious information management, yet unapt to enlist available computer power, the essential modern requisite in dealing with complexity. A paradigm shift to challenge the faulty ways by which complex systems in AEC domain are now addressed is overdue. This paper describes how the attributes and the application of an advanced design methodology – provisionally named Ravnikar Soper Technology (RST) – provide a powerful computational alternative.

Keywords: architecture, engineering, design, complexity, complex systems, CAD

1. Introduction

A signal objective of contemporary architectural design is delivery of fully operational computational methods capable of handling the steadily increasing complexity of engineered artefacts (Aish, Woodbury 2005, pp. 151–162; Bittermann 2009; Gürsel 2012, pp. 207–224; Herr 2002; Sánchez 2011; Yahiaoui et al. 2006, pp. 11–CD). In this perspective *complexity* is a subjective measure of difficulty in creating either the artefact itself or describing the process of its design. This inherent characteristic of the artefact/process represents the void between knowledge of components and knowledge of their compounded behaviour in cases of insufficient predictability of the output (Northrop 2010).

Architectural artefacts and even more their digital representations as result of evolutionary design process are regularly referred to as *complex systems*. These consist of subsystems and parts, whose internal organisation and connectivity to their surroundings cannot be described in simple terms (Sánchez 2011).

According to Luzeaux (2013) three main characteristics define a complex system: a) its elements respond to stimuli from adjacent elements, b) it is composed of a vast number of mostly heterogeneous units and c) interweaving of components is such that the general global structure and its behaviour cannot be deduced solely from the knowledge of particular local structures and their behaviour. Meier & Rechtin define *complex* as "composed of interconnected or interwoven parts" and *system* as "set of different elements so connected or related as to perform a unique function not performable by the elements alone". (Maier, Eberhardt 2009) Both architectural (Schmidt 2004, pp. 349–408) and engineering design (De Weck et al. 2011) are consistent with these qualifications, being complex systems themselves.

When large engineering assets are at stake (building construction among the largest) promoters expect careful, failure-proof, well planned-out ways of execution of projects, plus their guaranteed outcome. Or so they should. However, in the complex modern world, in the absence of methods that move with the times, such is more and more a self-defeating travail (Bar-Yam 2004). As the number of active elements in engineered systems – architectural artefacts included – as well as real-time demands on them keep increasing, highly complex design and subsequent engineering require new insights and new tools to tackle the growing complexity of these structures (Bar-Yam 2005, pp. 16–31).

Construction – consistently with systems engineering – is now primarily about separating large, highly complex plans, into smaller segments for distribution to various subcontractors to work on and coordinate their development so that the results of thus allotted pieces of the action can be effectively assembled at the end of the process. This schema of disassembly of global systems into sections is applied recursively into smaller and smaller parts until bits are sufficiently simple for single operators (men or machines) to implement and inversely to assemble the parts to integrate the entire system into a working order. The problem with this approach, however, is that it requires guidance in the distribution of tasks and coordination of assembly. Such sufficed in the past when projects were simpler. As they become more and more complex the process exposes its deficiencies until it breaks down (Bar-Yam 2004).

Eventually people get proficient at engineering systems in a typical, predictable manner, yet at the execution of complex and diversified projects, this principle increasingly fails (Bar-Yam 2004). With building design steadily growing more complex, breakdown happens earlier and earlier in the process. The larger the building, the higher its actual complexity, the sooner the malfunction occurs. To avoid aforesaid situation simplification, as aimed at reduction of complexity, is applied. In practice at a certain point where such approach is no longer feasible, yet the system's complexity still intractable, partly resolved design solutions are passed on to building contractors for further impoverishment in the course of their in-house provision of executive blueprints and shop drawings.

The most efficient way of handling complex systems in engineering design as everywhere else is by computer power (computationally). The problem of current CAD methods in tackling complexity is their incapacity of manipulation of more than a limited number of geometric entities. This is for two main reasons. One is the vast amount of geometric data and interrelations between them. The other is a geometric constraints problem (Hoffmann, Vermeer 1994, pp. 266–298; Thierry et al. 2009, pp. 1234–1249), a consequence of the former. With conventional CAD/BIM[1] relying on pre-rationalization[2] of design and geometric constraints, the growing complexity in the object of design overwhelms its progress, slowing it down

---

1 CAD/BIM – Computer Aided Design / Building Information Modelling (also Management).
2 Pre-rationalization means all relations between building constituents be considered in advance to so prevent problems slipping by and ensure the consistency of the model. This being impossible with very complicated and complex structures, there are, at the present, two routines of circumventing the problem. The first is to simplify the scheme, multiply layouts, and repeat components or parts. The second is to assign geometric and dimensional constraints to the constituent elements. Since there are so many constraints necessary to capture relations in a complex setup, such models quickly become over-constrained, with too many mutual dependencies; hence such CAD systems do not satisfy the listed conditions. This in turn is compensated by further simplification resulting in not nearly sufficient constraints being assigned for the design intent to be captured. Thus with its growing size the model gets increasingly under-constrained.

until it halts. Since, as said, this occurs unacceptably early in the process, the conventional systems, unfit to address complexity, spuriously reduce it in order to proceed. Simplification, repetition and imposition of staple library components together with regimented constraints pre-imposed on design models, deprive conventional CAD platforms of flexibility, necessary for production of complete information on the totality of building parts, fit for management of fabrication machinery.

Why it is that AEC hangs on to these dated methods of information management in construction? Part of the answer lies in past experience with strategies that worked for centuries. The present awareness that such no longer work exacts new design principles and tools, however. Some have attempted to address the issue of complexity by what has been termed generative design, which efforts, geared to serve specific purposes, eventually proved unfit for complex engineering, while other initiatives insist on systemic decrement of complexity of design, striving to apply to this pragmatism the stamp of method. Building information modelling, representative of the latter, aimed at remedying the current situation, is still laden with the conventional CAD paradigm, whose logic decrees that the larger a scheme, the more one should rely – in keeping it together – on reduction and simplification of its combined contents as well as components, greater size thus growing simpler not more complex. Functional issues of building design exact the very opposite, namely flawless information on non-uniform (also pseudo-regular[3]) uncurtailed complexity, whose degree of articulation increases with size.

To overcome the stalemate a paradigm change is essential. RST with its patented features effectively handles complexity on the path of its growth so to, in abrogation of recourse to facilitation through uniformity and regressive articulation, preserve complete information throughout the process of

---

Pre-rationalization is better known as 'comprehensive advance planning'. (Bar-Yam Y 2004)

3   Pseudo-regular constructs fare best in solving of architectural problems. They are most welcome whenever functional inflections of spatial concepts are required to match the complexities of multifarious building programmes. In reification of structures that solve architectural problems, complex pseudo-regular patterns are inevitable, however, to be feasible they must be handled as efficiently as regular ones, RST renders that possible.

open variation of possible solutions as precondition for selective guidance of complex development.

2. RST Approach

Development of architectural objects in ways introduced in this paper is a novel approach (Ravnikar, Šoper 2012), the culmination of work started in the 1970's (Ravnikar, Kmet 1971, pp. 93–128), with theoretical foundations outlined in 1982 (Ravnikar 1982). Experimental implementation had to wait until sufficiently capable computing equipment became readily affordable.

The general objective of engineering design is creation of data necessary for full description of physical objects to be fabricated. On top of satisfying this objective, RST achieves the additional goal of variability. Variability is signally important in design of complex objects, qua ability to concurrently explore multiple solutions and implement changes at any stage of object evolution. Owing to the complexity of considered solutions it is the normal requirement that continuous change be possible at any stage before the initial concept is finalized. With RST's design technique that is easily done.

A defining property of a complex object being our inability to predict its behaviour in advance and with pre-rationalization ruled out, another approach is necessary. We have, for the purposes of RST, adopted a generalized Darwinist procedure as summarized in the BVSR principles, first introduced by D. Campbell (Boyd 2009, pp. 26–28; Campbell 1974, pp. 139–161) to provide the design method with a theoretical framework.

RST stems from two principles: *causality* and *locality*. The former determines that each new state of a system is a causal derivation of a previous state in an arbitrarily long series of events. The latter dictates that the parameters of each operation in the system are defined by relative paths, regarding an object O over which the operation is executed. Results of operations are added as new objects related to O. In RST, all objects are manipulated by the graph data structure, which we describe in the sequel.

2.1 The Structure of the System

In RST a description of object's geometry, its composition and the procedure describing its creation is called *model*. With objects composed of different parts, the model must have a description for each of its parts plus informa- tion about how these are to be put together (their connectivity reflected in relative positions and assembly procedures). All information about the model is stored in a graph data structure called *model graph* **G**. RST uses the model graph not only to store model data (information describing the model), but also information describing the design process itself, its steps, its parameters and their relations.

Each vertex in **G** contains either information about placeholders repre- senting the shape of the model, abstract objects suggesting design concepts (floor, roof, window, ...), auxiliary geometry objects (point, line, plane, intermediate solid object, etc.) or information about the atomic parts (the final, indivisible parts of the model).

Two vertices in **G** are connected by a directed edge if their contents are in some (logical or physical) relation within the model; e.g. vertices representing adjacent placeholders for two neighbouring components are connected by an edge. Each edge in **G** is assigned an attribute 'name'. Dur- ing the process new vertices are inserted into graph data structure so that eventually every part of the model is added in **G** as content of some vertex.

RST model is generated using three main operations: *generator, selector, task*.

Generators are functions inputted by sets of parameters that create new vertices in **G,** usually with accompanying geometric primitives or placehold- ers representing abstract structure. Numbers and types of external param- eters depend on types of generating functions. For example, a *sine* function may be given three parameters: argument, phase and scale. The generating function must be provided with a discrete variable, either through explicit parameter or through ordered selection of vertices from **G** when used as parameters. Each generated content is then assigned a different label, usu- ally an integer.

Selectors are functions that identify subsets of vertices from **G**, such that they (or their contents) satisfy given conditions; e.g. value of a certain attribute is greater than a defined parameter or a vertex is incident to an edge with a given name, etc. Sets of vertices returned by selectors are *selec- tions*. Selectors mainly identify patterns or subsets of vertices representing concepts.

Tasks are functions that take various parameters (numerical, textual, and functional), as well as vertices of **G**, specified exclusively by relative paths, as inputs. Tasks are executed upon all vertices of a given selection, referred to as *working selection*. Outputs are new vertices of **G** together with their contents. Vertices of **G**, given as inputs to tasks, are reminiscent of constraints (the fons et origo of ineffectual coping with complexity) in conventional CAD/parametric systems. With RST complexity is simplified (but not reduced) by adoption of locality principle and by avoidance of cyclical dependencies.

2.2 Model Construction

Here we describe the method of constructing a model. In **Figure 1** a diagram of the process is represented.

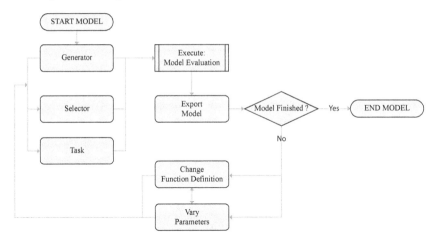

Figure 1: Flow chart diagram of RST approach.

STEP 1: The first step defines the initial graph of the underlying logical structure as the original state of **G**. Experimental work has shown that initial structures need not be elaborate. It suffices to start with simple, well-understood graphs; e.g. paths, planar or toroidal grids etc. or arbitrary meshes.

The logical structure initiates the partition of design space into logical units. For example, in a high-rise building model, the logical structure would reflect a generally accepted rule that such a tower is primarily organized as a set of floors on top of one another. The logical structure graph representing such an arrangement is a list of vertices, each representing a floor. The vertices representing adjacent floors are connected by an edge. Obviously all vertices have two neighbours, a floor below and a floor above, except the first and the last one. An example of a logical-structure graph is shown in **Figure 2**.

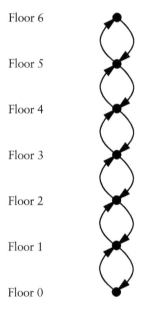

| Floor 6 |
| Floor 5 |
| Floor 4 |
| Floor 3 |
| Floor 2 |
| Floor 1 |
| Floor 0 |

Figure 2: Logical structure graph of a building with 7 floors.

STEP 2: Preliminary logical structure created in the first step is a precondition for following operations on the model in next stages of the RST procedure. According to the BVSR approach, using generators and varying their parameters, a number of initial representations of the model are created. Arbitrary variation of parameters can produce unexpected, emergent results that may have radically different geometric representations, while the underlying structure – the *model graph* – stays the same; its topology remains unchanged from variation to variation. Emergent features represent considerable, essentially insurmountable problems for conventional CAD applications. RST handles them easily, since the underlying structure is sustained regardless of variation. The designer can either select or define its features in the terms of graph structure without recourse to geometric quantities.

Among an infinite number of different shapes there will be such that match conditions of a design brief. This shifts the focus from pre-rationalising of solutions to discovering them, as phenomena are discovered in nature.

Figure 3: Variations of a high-rise building shape all derived from the same logical (underlying) structure.

STEP 3: With the shape of a model defined we proceed to construction of feature placeholders, which, after many refinements, will be transformed into fully resolved objects of the model. In particular, when constructing an atomic part of the model, we define a number of sequences of tasks and execute them upon selections. Arbitrarily long sequences of tasks may be defined, since – owing to locality and acyclicity – the complexity of execution remains at the same level throughout the process.

Above described steps are not disjoined. Additional vertices representing a logical structure may therefore be added at any stage of modelling as well as new generating functions and additional tasks applied to selections.

2.3 Model Evaluation

The concepts proposed in a design process are abstract, and may be extracted from operations performed in the *model graph*. Operations are defined in a script language interpreted by the execution engine (see Figure 4). Execution of generators and selectors is straightforward, since they perform upon sets of vertices of *G* without further dependencies.

Tasks, on the other hand, are substantially more demanding owing to simultaneous interdependencies within the model graph. The number of these is usually much greater than the number of generators and selectors. For instance, there are tens of thousands of tasks executed in a design of a major building, while only several hundred selectors and few generators may be defined.

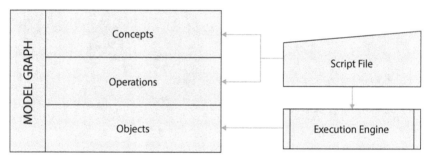

Figure 4: Data model of RST approach.

Tasks are defined in the RST script language. The order of their definitions can be arbitrary, since ordering is handled by the execution engine. A task is executed only after the objects it depends on are already created, i.e. inserted in *G*. Therefore, tasks are performed in such order that a task *T* is executed in sequel to all tasks that create objects which *T* receives as input parameters.

Consequent to the nature of task definition, such an ordering is altogether possible. It is carried out in an acyclic directed graph, which we refer to as the *dependency graph* *D* of the model. Vertices in *D* represent tasks while two tasks, *T* and *U*, are connected by a directed edge *(T,U)* if the output of *T* is a parameter of *U*. Obviously, the task *U* is executed after each task from which a directed path goes to *U* has finished the execution – we say that *U depends on T*. Since every task *T* is executed at every vertex *v* of a given working selection, there is a check whether all objects prescribed as parameters to *T* were created on the relative paths from *v*. If not, the task is not executed at *v*.

RST creation of objects in a model thus enables a high degree of parallelization. In particular, execution of a task can be divided into as many processes as is the size of its working selection. Additionally, any pair of independent tasks in *D*, with all the tasks they depend on already done, may be executed in parallel.

3. Conclusion

We have introduced a design methodology that solves many problems of modern building design and construction, which other design initiatives fail to address. Our process results in fully resolved models of highly complex objects, delivering complete geometric, material and any other required information for each and every part of the designed object.

In **Figure 5** an example of detailed construction of hanging curtain façade elements with connecting components is shown. It was done by computation exclusively.

Figure 5: Construction of a complex curtain façade.

By the logic of this novel approach to the design of complex objects, we managed to bypass the pitfalls of standard constraining techniques and cross-dependencies within sets of constraints in conventional digital models. Adherence to causality and locality rules enables RST to pass from attempts at tackling of insoluble systems of constraints to solution of multiple independent ones, individually for each part of the model. Causality warrants non-circular dependencies between constraints, while locality ensures only locally polynomial computational complexity in the evaluation of constraints. Since maximum number of local constraints for each part in the model is small, the overall complexity of solving constraints is asymptotically linear in the number of parts in a model. Linearity thus enables RST to scale progressively and naturally with size.

Some will argue that for such results too much is paid by giving away the coordination of the overall model. In answer to that we point at another quality of RST, strict maintenance of model graph – the abstract, logical structure of the whole model, which coordinates every operation.

A further important advantage of RST is highly parallelizable execution plan for model evaluation. Again, locality principle ensures that each operation depends only on a small number of previously created objects in the model, so that any number of disparate parts of the model can be evaluated in parallel. Another advantage is that each atomic operation merely demands modest computing resources, while the bulk of the model resides on secondary storage. RST is thus perfectly fit for clusters of low-powered standard computers and for usage in on-demand cloud solutions.

Given the fact that our design procedure is independent of the domain (3D artefacts to be industrially manufactured), this procedure can also be implemented in other domains where complexities arise, such as knowledge management, expert systems, computer programming and the like.

List of references

Aish, Robert / Woodbury, Robert: "Multi-level Interaction in Parametric Design". In: Butz, A. et al. (eds.): *SmartGraphics, 5th International Symposium*, LNCS 3638. Springer Verlag: Berlin Heidelberg 2005, pp. 151–162.

Bar-Yam, Yaneer: "About Engineering Complex Systems: Multiscale Analysis and Evolutionary Engineering". In: Brueckner, S. et al. (eds.): *ESOA 2004*, LNCS 3464. Springer Verlag: Berlin Heidelberg 2005, pp. 16–31.

Bar-Yam, Yaneer: *Making things Work – Solving complex problems in a complex world*. NECSI Knowledge Press: Cambridge 2004.

Bittermann, Michael S.: *Intelligent Design Objects (IDO): a cognitive approach for performance-based design* (doctoral thesis). Delft University of Technology: Delft 2009.

Boyd, Brian: "Purpose-Driven Life". *The American Scholar*, Spring 2009, pp. 26–28.

Campbell, Donald T.: "Unjustified variation and selective retention in scientific discovery". In: Ayala, F. / Dobzhansky, T. (eds.): *Studies in the Philosophy of Biology*. University of California Press: Los Angeles 1974, pp. 139–161.

De Weck, Olivier L. / Roos, Daniel / Magee, Christopher L.: *Engineering Systems: Meeting Human Needs in a Complex Technological World*. MIT Press: Cambridge 2011.

Gürsel, Dino I.: "Creative design by parametric generative systems". *METU Journal of the Faculty of Architecture* 29(1), 2012, pp. 207–224.

Herr, Christiane M.: "Generative Architectural Design and Complexity Theory". In: *Generative Art 2002: 5th International Generative Art Conference GA2002*, Milan 2002.

Hoffmann, Christoph M. / Vermeer, P. J.: "Geometric constraint solving in R2 and R3". In: Du, D. Z. / Huang, F. (eds.): *Computing in Euclidean Geometry*. World Scientific: Singapore 1994, pp. 266–298.

Luzeaux, Dominique: "Engineering Large-scale Complex Systems". In: Luzeaux D. et al. (eds.): *Complex Systems and Systems of Systems Engineering*. John Wiley & Sons: Hoboken NJ 2013.

Maier, Mark W. / Rechtin, Eberhardt: *The Art of Systems Architecting (3rd edition)*. CRC Press: USA 2009.

Northrop, Robert B.: *Introduction to Complexity and Complex Systems*. CRC Press: Boca Raton 2010.

Ravnikar, Edo: "Tracciato morfogenetico dello sviluppo del manufatto". In: Padovano G. (ed.): *Territorio e Architettura: Metodologie sceintifiche nell'analisi e nell'intervento*. Etas Libri: Milan 1982.

Ravnikar, Edo / Kmet, Andrej: "Propositions: Esquisse d'une theorie de la projetation". *NEUF* 30, 1971, pp. 93–128.

Ravnikar, E. / Šoper, R.: Method and apparatus for computer-aided design of three-dimensional objects to be fabricated, US Patent 8,103,484, 2012.

Sánchez, Vibaek K.: *System structures in architecture* (doctoral thesis). Centre for Industrialised Architecture, The Royal Danish Academy of Fine Arts, School of Architecture: Copenhagen 2011.

Schmidt, Kjeld / Wagner, Ina: "Ordering Systems: Coordinative Practices and Artifacts in Architectural Design and Planning". *Computer Supported Cooperative Work* 13, 2004, pp. 349–408.

Thierry, Simon E. B. / Schreck, Pascal / Michelucci, Dominique / Fünfzig, Christoph / Génevaux, Jean-David: "Extensions of the witness method to characterize under-, over- and well-constrained geometric constraint systems". *Computer-Aided Design* 43, 2011, pp. 1234–1249.

Yahiaoui, Azzedine / Sahraoui, Abd-El-Kader / Hensen, Jan / Brouwer, Paul: "A systems engineering environment for integrated building design". In: *Proceedings of the EuSEC – European Systems Engineering Conf.*, Edinburgh 2006, pp. 11–CD.

Igor Bernik
Faculty of Criminal Justice and Security, University of Maribor
Kotnikova 8, 1000 Ljubljana, Slovenia
igor.bernik@fvv.uni-mb.si

Cybercrime: what we know about perpetrators

Abstract: The understanding of perpetrators, their motives and ways in which they organize themselves in order to commit acts of abuse in cyberspace is one of the aspects in the fight against cybercrime. Since contemporary users and the manner of conducting business became completely dependent on technology, networking and information exchange, all our activities are now prone to potential abuse. Adopting preventive measures and taking into account principles related to cyber security are the best defence against abuse. In order to carry out law enforcement and prosecution activities in the field of cybercrime, which is global in its very nature, it is necessary to reach consensus at the international level, thus providing the basis for joint activities to be performed by entities and persons under attack, law enforcement authorities and the judiciary, so that perpetrators would recognize their acts as undesirable and unacceptable in a modern, always on-always connected society.

Keywords: cybercrime, perpetrators, motives, organization

1. Introduction

Cyberspace, characterized by multidimensional connections, varied hardware and services, represents a global environment of interoperability, information exchange in the business world, companies' operation, interorganizational and consumer cooperation, as well as social interactions. Such an environment requires the transmission of vast volumes of data that must be provided with an adequate level of security due to their quantity, different forms of transfer and the complexity of relevant technology, which is difficult to achieve, but necessary from the business point of view. Since technological safety features and protective mechanisms are extremely sophisticated, the majority of cases related to the abuse of data take place by attacking end users' devices or end users themselves or by exploiting security gaps of hardware and, more frequently, software in order to obtain the desired data. There are several ways to obtain the desired data and cybercrime perpetrators are continuously coming up with new, innovative and advances methods. In terms of protection, the following general rule applies: in order to decrease attacks and consequences of cybercrime, one must increase the time necessary for attackers to obtain the desired data and presume that they will give up before obtaining such data. However, when attackers are driven by a specific motive, they will obtain the desired data from the system no matter how safe and secure it is, since no one can provide complete (cyber) security, particularly in the global cyberspace.

Despite the general view that cybercrime emerged in recent years with the increasing use of the Internet, it has to be pointed out that it was already present in the past. It developed together with cyberspace and ICT. Its scope extended in parallel with the development of technology. Cybercrime perpetrators are becoming more experienced every day and use a number of techniques that are relatively unknown to the regular cyberspace users, which forces knowledge and defense systems to always be one step behind the attackers. In particular, the integrity, care, and handling of basics cybersecurity measures as an unfinished process and can be the only defense against information and security incidents. The main cause of this is the global orientation of cyberspace, the ambiguity of legal norms and the possibility to transfer illegal activities to parts of the world where they are allowed, or where the perpetrators are simply not prosecuted. Crimes in cyberspace are characterized by the fact that the damage caused is unclear and it is difficult to determine its financial consequences.

Electronic devices, which interconnect and transfer data to or through the Internet are just an additional tool for the perpetrators, an accessory to commit criminal offenses in cyberspace. The Internet gives them a global dimension, enables them to stay anonymous and communicate directly and safely, opens the way to knowledge, generates a large number of victims, and gives a plethora of opportunities and assistance for carrying out illegal transactions.

In the overall treatment of cybercrime there are still problems related to the corroboration of attacks, the cause of damage, and the identification of perpetrators, which is why many such acts remain unreported, unpursued, and the perpetrators at large (Wall 2008, p. 46). Global vulnerability of the "networked" society can be observed in numerous cases of data theft, online fraud, the spreading of malware, and inoperative systems, as well as in the amount of estimated loss, which is measured in millions ((IC3 2011, p. 4), (Ponemon 2012, pp. 7–8)). The number of perpetrators of cybercrime as well as the damage they cause is constantly growing. In 2000, Gartner predicted a 1,000 % increase in damage over the next four years (Dimetriou 2003, p. 215). For these reasons almost ten years later Dobovšek (2009, p. 471) notes that cybercrime can "easily be ranked among the most dangerous and socially most harmful forms of modern crime". A much appreciated characteristic of the Internet, i.e. the ability to hide or misrepresent one's identity, is the main reason for such a situation. The Internet enables everyone to be whoever they want to be online, which means that it is relatively difficult to detect the true identity of the person who has, for example, stolen credit card numbers from the bank or attacked a website and thus prevented its functioning.

Perpetrators of cybercrime are well versed in and able to properly hide their identity, so that investigators are unable to discover who carries out the offenses. Finding the perpetrators in cyberspace may seem very easy to laymen and those unaware of network technologies. In reality, however, the complexity of technology and the global nature of cyberspace make their detection extremely difficult. The situation related to the spread of cybercrime in recent years became even worse due to more sophisticated methods of attack and refined forms of misuse, large numbers of users, and cases of identity misuse. The development of computer technology and the emergence of communication between computers showed, in the 1980s, that when individuals who communicate with each other do not know each other (are anonymous), the phenomenon of deindividuation may appear, resulting in an increasingly anti-social behaviour. When deindividuated, an individual cannot control their own behaviour anymore due to perceived anonymity. The latest version of the deindividuation theory – Social Identity Theory of Deindividuation (SIDE) – argues that the personality is divided into two parts: personal identity with individual characteristics, and social identity, which comes to the fore in a particular group. Individuals will behave in a deviant way, if their social or group identity support and encourage this kind of behaviour and vice versa (Williams 2008, p. 148).

Perhaps users feel "hidden" among so many other people or believe they are immersed in the vast cyberspace, made up of millions of users connected to the Internet. They see themselves more as a part of this large group than as individuals. They are aware of the relative distance from others and relative immunity from the identification and sanctions. An individual in cyberspace is also "deaf" or is not aware of the significance of their acts and their consequences in the real world. Anonymity and deindividuation play a certain role in the decision of an individual to carry out criminal offenses. The anonymity and deindividuation of cyberspace users alone are not the causes of deviant behaviour, but can encourage individuals, who are already inclined to do so for one reason or another, to engage in such acts. Williams (2008, p. 154) believes that there would be a lot more crime if anonymity in itself caused deviant behaviour. Although it seems that anonymity causes cybercrime; in reality, however, it is nothing else but a rational choice for those who are already predisposed to crime or deviant behaviour. Regardless of the type of crime, its basis is certainly to maintain anonymity. Irrespective of the fact that someone acts as a pirate or a hacker, the offenses of both stem from the assumption that the discovery of their identity by the authorities is not very likely. If one also considers the commitment of authorities to prosecute this type of crime, one could observe that the fear of possible sanctions is almost nonexistent. The combination of anonymity and low probability of sanctions is certainly the reason for individual forms of crime, which directly impair a certain person or more persons, an organization, or even a country. Therefore, it seems that the role of anonymity and deindividuation in cybercrime cannot be viewed separately, which is somehow logical due to so many different forms of cybercrime. Some experts understand anonymity and deindividuation as the cause, while others believe it acts as a kind of catalyst. Given the fact that cybercrime is rapidly increasing, the aforementioned factors certainly play an important role, although this type of crime is not yet precisely defined and studied.

The methods of attacks vary considerably in terms of risk, costs, and complexity. The perpetrators often prefer to choose low risk and thus lower revenues from their criminal offenses. The amount of revenues is one of the measures on the basis of which offenders can be classified, but it has to be noted that there are also large differences in the way they are organized.

It could be stated that the better the perpetrators are organized, interconnected, and the more assets they invest, the greater their profits.

The prosecution of criminal offenses in cyberspace is problematic, as it is always necessary to adapt the methods of detection, investigation, and guaranteeing proof. Apart from that, people even decide not to report many cybercrime offenses. Often they do so because they completely overlook the offenses or believe that they are to blame for the abuse. Organizations that have often been abused believe that in order to protect their reputation and confidence in their operations it is futile to report cyber attacks, their potential damage or consequences. They thus additionally contribute to the growth of cybercrime, since the perpetrators do not feel at risk at all.

2. Cybercrime Perpetrators

Perpetrators committing fraud are mostly collecting financial assets of uninformed or careless users by acquiring confidential information and then blackmailing them or by stealing money from their bank accounts. There are many programs developed to combat this type of attacks, but cybercrime perpetrators are already so skillful that no user protection program can stop them. In the future the number of attacks will only increase, and new technologies and methods for committing cybercrime will be developed (UNODC 2011, p. 203). In the past, the main motive of perpetrators was to prove that no system is completely secure, because each of them has critical points, which perpetrators are able to detect and abuse the possibility of intrusion. Initially, the main motive of cybercrime perpetrators was amusement, curiosity, etc., while today they operate primarily for profit or money they obtain from data and identity thefts, while the majority of attacks directly enable the gain of financial resources, especially from online fraud. It could, therefore, be said that most crimes committed in cyberspace today are financially conditioned.

2.1 Motives

The motivation of the offenders to commit a criminal offense differs from person to person; they may want to obtain reputation, self-confirmation, revenge, and most often financial gains. We must not forget that cyberspace is an effective weapon in the hands of terrorists, politically motivated individuals and groups, and increasingly organized crime groups. Among others, active users and dealers of child pornography are also on the internet. The IC3 report for 2010 (IC3 2010, p. 11) shows that most cybercrime originates from the United States (65.9 %), followed by the United Kingdom (10.4 %), Nigeria (5.8 %), China (3.1 %) and Canada (2.4 %), which is contrary to the basic presumption that the majority of perpetrators originate from countries, where the probability of prosecution is low and commit their criminal acts in global cyberspace. Nevertheless, studies indicate that organized cybercrime is migrating from the aforementioned developed countries to areas, which are less developed in terms of cybercrime prosecution, as well as in terms of their regulatory framework and economic performance. According to recent studies, the most common purpose of cybercrime perpetrators is to obtain financial benefits (e.g. (Ponemon 2011, p. 1), Ponemon 2012, p. 27) and (Trustwave 2013, p. 62)), which result in large financial losses, especially for companies. Also, the data of identified offenders and other studies (e.g. Gartnergroup 2011, p. 4) suggest that the motives of perpetrators range from (self)confirmation to obtaining material benefits. The main motive of perpetrators is thus a desire to make money, and this is also the main cause of modern cybercrime, especially identity theft, the use of spam, installing or running of botnets with information gathering from the infected devices and the production of malware, which is installed on users' devices to take control over such devices and obtain the desired data.

Since cybercrime today is no longer a game played by computer geeks, but a profitable criminal affair, it is necessary to behave carefully and take into account both technical and user tips and techniques to reduce exposure and risks when participating in cyberspace. As the motives of perpetrators are very different, the aforementioned factors are difficult to avoid.

2.2 Types of Offenders

Just as regular criminal offenses are committed by individuals or groups, cyberspace is also populated with individuals or groups that we are oblivious to because they use the ICT. Nevertheless, one must not forget that a human being is responsible for every action in cyberspace. When it comes to "classic" criminal offenses people have an idea of the actual perpetrator, but when it comes to cyber perpetrators, we somehow lose this actual image or do not even create one. It would thus be useful to start profiling cyber criminals and get to know their organization, just as this is done with the perpetrators of classic criminal offenses. This would help to dispel the myths and preconceptions that society and legislators have regarding cyber criminals. Many perpetrators of cybercrime are professional people who use their knowledge to achieve various goals. A study (Bernik and Meško 2011, pp. 242–252) showed that a classic stereotype of a young hacker who spends all their time in front of a computer and is not interested in their social environment is no longer true. A generic term used by the public for people who commit cybercrime is a hacker, but the subculture of perpetrators is much more divided and complex. There are several subgroups of offenders, which are divided according to different criteria: e.g. by their level of technical knowledge, field of interest, and the use and knowledge of software and hardware. These subgroups are further divided into more narrow categories. A division into seven basic categories is proposed (Chiesa and Ducci 2009, p. 162):

- Toolkit newbies; novices who only have little technical skills, use ready-made software and follow the documentation to guide them through the procedures of the programs.
- Cyber Punks; create small programs that are used for defacing, spamming, or stealing credit card details.
- Internals; employees or former employees who seek revenge; their main goal is to damage the system of the company, and use the knowledge they have with regard to the security situation within the organization rather than technical knowledge.
- Coders; the creators of codes designed to damage other systems.
- Old-guard hackers, hackers in short; have a high level of expertise and mostly do not have criminal intentions. They are more interested in the intellectual and cognitive side of hacking.
- Professionals; the most dangerous perpetrators of cybercrime. Their goal is always criminal in nature.

Even in the hacker underground there are good and bad "players". In this respect it is possible to distinguish between the following types of offenders (Chiesa and Ducci 2009, p. 165):

- Black-hats; the name suggests that they are baddies who commit illegal acts, and their main purpose is to harm information systems, steal information, etc.
- Grey-hats; the so-called ethical hackers who do not want to belong to neither bad nor good ones. In the past, some of them might have even dealt with the intrusion into information systems, but have decided to stop such practice.
- White-hats; have the knowledge and skills that would enable them to function in the same way as black-hats, but they decided to be on the right side of the law. To this end, they often cooperate with the authorities and companies, and work with them in order to combat cybercrime. In the past, they rarely engaged in illegal attacks on information systems.

According to the classification described, there are only three main groups, but e.g. black-hats can be further divided into various sub-groups, such as basic coders, script kiddies, firebug hackers, legal black hackers and others. In the criminal underworld there are many other classifications and terms that designate a particular type of cybercrime perpetrators. The most commonly known (Chiesa and Ducci 2009, p. 164) are: wannabe lamer, cracker, ethical hacker, cyber-warrior, industrial spy, government agent, etc. These individual types of perpetrators often come together in different groups and organizations in order to pool their knowledge and resources, thus guaranteeing maximum profitability of their activities and causing tremendous losses to individuals and organizations under attack.

2.3 Perpetrators Organization

When referring to the knowledge of perpetrators, the author makes reference to a detailed analysis of their way of thinking, method of operation, lifestyle, motives that lead them to commit crimes, and their organization. The research into and understanding of these topics, in particular, can be the greatest advantage in identifying the perpetrators. Today's offenders are most often organized into different groups, which are interconnected. This ensures that the application of knowledge converges towards the common goal of the group; mostly this involves the unlawful acquisition of benefits or public visibility of actions. In the past, cyber criminals operated independently. They created their own hacking tools, invaded systems, created their own phishing pages that would send spam by themselves, steal bank account information, etc. Modern perpetrators are better organized, more connected, and have advanced knowledge (Wall 2008, p. 47). Several research studies were made, which analysed the method of operation of crime groups in cyberspace, which includes the following members (Web Security Trends Report 2013, p. 6):

- The Boss is the head of the organization. He operates as a business entrepreneur and doesn't commit the (cyber)crimes himself.
- Directly under The Boss is the Underboss acting as the second in command and managing the operation. In case of cybercrime, he is the one that provides the Trojans for attacks and manages the Command and Control (C&C) of those Trojans.
- Beneath the underboss as lieutenants leading their own section of the operation, Campaign managers lead their own attack campaigns. They use their own "affiliation networks" to perform the attacks and steal the data.
- The stolen data are sold by Resellers. These resellers are not involved in the Crimeware attacks, but trade the stolen data similar to a "fence" dealing with stolen goods.

The organizational structure of these groups is comparable to the organizational structure of the mafia (e.g. (Dobovšek 2009, p. 447), (Web Security Trends Report 2013, pp. 6–7)). The same situation that characterized the mafia in the past, is now characteristic of the cybercrime perpetrators' subculture; an individual approach to cybercrime is replaced by the system of organizations which reflect the hierarchical structure typical of the mafia.

With the transition of cybercrime from amateur hacker attacks to highly professional cybercrime business models, we see that the organizational structure of cyber criminals reflects mentioned trend. Individual hackers operating independently or groups of hackers with common goals have been replaced by hierarchical cybercrime organizations were each cybercriminal has his own well defined role and reward system. The current cybercrime organizations bear an uncanny resemblance to organized crime organization. (Web Security Trends Report 2013, p. 2)

The websites on which they carry out their unlawful activities (dissemination of child pornography, illegal sale of copyrighted works, etc.) are usually placed on servers in countries with inadequate laws, no international agreements and with less qualified law enforcement authorities. Such problematic areas mainly include South America, Africa and some less developed countries of Eastern Europe and the former Soviet Union. Perpetrators of crime in cyberspace pursue the same objectives and operate under the same influences as the perpetrators of traditional forms of crime. Since the modern cybercrime is characterized by highly experienced criminal groups, it is necessary to choose an appropriate protection against attacks in order to ensure the appropriate level of security.

3. Discussion

Undoubtedly, the environment in which the perpetrator acts is an important factor of crime. The characteristics of cyberspace, in which an offense takes place, are extremely varied. When planning and implementing measures to restore cybersecurity it is beneficial to understand and follow the guidelines of situational prevention. Security measures taken by organizations or countries at the entry points into their own IT environment certainly affect the decision of the offender. The architectural strategy is thus a very appropriate measure to deter malicious users of ICT. The greater the effort the offender must invest, and the longer the time that must be spent to overcome security obstacles, the less likely it is for the offender to decide to carry out a criminal act. Therefore, organizations and countries must provide for the establishment of a multifaceted strategy for cybersecurity. The higher the number of protective mechanisms which overlap and prevent perpetrators unauthorized access to the system, the lower is the likelihood for the offender to decide to invade. The combination of the quantity and quality of the measures is, of course, very important. It is the perpetrator, who we wish to influence by changing cyberspace. The best solution for the prevention of cybercrime is to extend the perpetrator's time and effort needed to achieve their goal and to adopt relevant legislation, which increases the chance of detection and conviction of offenders. Above all, the international community should reach consensus regarding what cybercrime actually is, establish adequate legal basis, bring the perpetrators to justice, sentence them for their crimes, and thus show that the fight against cybercrime is a fact and that crimes in cyberspace are not worth committing. It is also important for organizations to establish appropriate security policies, and constantly educate and inform users which have to be aware of the risks.

At the moment, cybercrime development and its threat to cyberspace users are increasing exponentially. It is also known that cybercrime is expanding its range of operation and attracting ever more organized, sophisticated, and covert perpetrators within its environment. Due to their political, economic, or ideological motivation these represent the greatest threat to society, since societal consequences of their actions are much more detrimental than the consequences of the traditional financially motivated cybercrime. In this context it is clear that the perpetrators of criminal acts are not waiting, but are extremely up-to-date, flexible, inconstant, and organized. It is precisely these attributes that law enforcement agencies, legislative acts, organizations, and countries should possess when countering threats in cyberspace. However, the current situation shows that the opposite holds true.

Therefore, a lot more will have to be done in order to diminish the impacts of cybercrime on persons using cyberspace services. However, experience shows that one can achieve a significant decrease in the number of successful attacks and abuse of data by taking some basic steps in the field of security and raising end users' awareness. Given the fact that one cannot expect immediate results in the field of defense against attacks and risk prevention simply by patiently awaiting the response of institutions and international organizations, and amending existing legislation, it is suggested that users put safety features and protective mechanisms, which are available for different technological devices and networks, to use and raise their awareness regarding potential threats and the identification of clandestine attacks. At the same time, users ought to be more skeptical when participating in unknown methods of communication, accepting seemingly unbeatable offers and kind words of those, who contact them via various communication channels (in person, by telephone, e-mail, online social networks) in order to obtain basic personal data, which are subsequently used to circumvent technological safety features and protective mechanisms, and abuse data owned or handled by individual users. By doing so, they will not only make the work of attackers more difficult, but also decrease their own exposure to such threats.

List of references

Bernik, Igor / Mesko, Gorazd: "Internetna študija poznavanja kibernetskih groženj in strahu pred kibernetsko kriminaliteto". *Revija za kriminalistiko in kriminologijo*, 62(3), 2011, pp. 242–252.

Chiesa, Raoul / Ducci, Stefania / Ciappi, Silvio: *Profiling Hackers. The Science of Criminal Profiling as Applied to the World of Hacking*. Auerbach Publications: New York 2009.

Demetriou, Christina / Silke, Andrew: "A Criminological Internet »Sting«: Experimental evidence of illegal and deviant visits to a website trap". *The British Journal of Criminology*, 43(1), 2003, pp. 213–222.

Dobovšek, Bojan., *Transnacionalna kriminaliteta*. Fakulteta za varnostne vede: Ljubljana 2009.

Gartnergroup: *Security Risk Management*, retrieved 29. 4. 2011 from http://www.gartner.com/technology/research/security-risk-management.jsp.

IC3: *Internet Crime Report Annual Report, NW3C – White Collar Crime Center*, retrieved 30.11.2010 from http://www.ic3.gov/media/annualreport/2010_ic3report.pdf.

IC3: *Internet Crime Report 2010 Internet Crime Report*, retrieved 28.10.2011 from http://www.ic3.gov/media/annualreport/2010_IC3Report.pdf.

Ponemon: *Second Annual Cost of Cyber Crime Study: Benchmark Study of U.S. Companies*, Ponemon Institute, Michigan 2011.

Ponemon: *2012 Cost of Cyber Crime Study: United States*, retrieved 3.3.2013 from http://www.ponemon.org/local/upload/file/2012_US_Cost_of_Cyber_Crime_Study_FINAL6%20.pdf.

Trustwave: *Trustwave 2013 Global Security Report*, retrieved 2.3.2013 from http://www2.trustwave.com/rs/trustwave/images/2013-Global-Security-Report.pdf.

UNODC: *The Globalization of Crime*, retrieved 3.12.2011 from https://www.unodc.org/documents/data-and-analysis/tocta/TOCTA_Report_2010_low_res.pdf.

Wall, David. S.: "Cybercrime, media and insecurity: the shaping of public perceptions of cybercrime". *International Review of Law, Computers and Technology*, 22(1–2), 2008, pp. 45–63.

Web Security Trends Report: *Finjan Malicious Code Research Center*, retrieved 2.3.2013 from https://www.incibe.es/file/whfcdjQColf5jJX CucHxhQ.

Williams, Katherine. S.: "Using Tittle's control balance theory to understand computer crime and deviance". *International Review of Law Computers & Technology*, 22(1–2), 2008, pp. 145–155.

Andrej Dobrovoljc
Faculty of Information Studies, Sevno 13, 8000 Novo mesto, Slovenia
andrej.dobrovoljc@fis.unm.si

Towards detection of malicious threats for information systems

Abstract: Risk assessment of information systems depends on recognized system vulnerabilities and detected threats. From the security assurance point of view it is essential to discover and remove vulnerabilities as soon as possible. Therefore, various Vulnerability Discovery Models (VDM) were proposed for making predictions about discoveries in software products. Since vulnerabilities without threats are not harmful, we should pay attention to prediction of malicious threats as well. We did not find any threat prediction models in the existing literature. Authors of malicious attacks are always people with bad intentions. Therefore, we should understand their behaviour and detect the moment when the system becomes attractive to them. Our intention in this paper was to uncover possibilities for making such predictions. We describe some possible approaches, which will be deeply examined in further studies.

Keywords: threat, discovery, risk, vulnerability, attacker, TAM

1. Introduction

It is very difficult to answer the question of how safe our information system (IS) is. Individuals daily discover new and unknown IS vulnerabilities, which allows new attacks and consequently sustains constant threat. With the IS globalization vulnerability discovery becoming extremely popular. Companies are forced to open their IS to the web in order to keep their competitiveness. Trade via Internet and all sorts of financial transactions were enormously increased in the last decade as well. All these changes attract criminals, who want to earn something out of it. The first step on the way to the successful exploitation of web applications or protocols is to find their vulnerabilities. By using them, attackers can develop and use various attacks against IS, which leads to huge economical and private financial damage.

Only highly skilled and innovative individuals can discover vulnerabilities. Due to this fact, the knowledge about undisclosed vulnerabilities becomes a respected merchandise. Today, we are aware of a real vulnerability market where the customers are criminal groups, terrorists, governments, specific private companies and other special groups. In order to avoid such trading, some initiatives require better quality of software products regarding their security. Others demand severe legislation against vendors, which would define their responsibility for security. The vulnerability market is a fact and we have to find some other preventive actions. We should not overlook the other important types of vulnerabilities. Information system does not consist only of software, but also of the other types of components. Among them, people are the weakest link and vulnerable to various malicious threats such as social engineering attacks and the like. Therefore, some specific risk mitigation mechanisms arose in the security ecosystem, which are mainly focused to vulnerability discovery, elimination, prediction and prevention.

However, security risks do not depend only on vulnerabilities. Until threat appears, there is no risk. Therefore, it is also important to discover possible future threats around the information system. Behind every malicious threat is a human. The question that we address in this paper is how we can anticipate the appearance of future malicious threats. The answer to this question can improve the risk assessment process, since it would allow the IS owner to mitigate risk in advance. In our study, we focused on attackers' behaviour as well as on their trails, which are recorded in various databases.

The remainder of this paper is structured as follows. Section two describes existing approaches for proactive security assurance. In the third section the opportunities for malicious threats detection are given. In the final section, a paper summary is given with a short description of the main ideas and plans for future work.

2. Related work

Information system security risk is calculated by the following formula (Eq. 1):

$$Risk = Vulnerability * Threat * AssetValue \text{ (1)}$$

Information system (IS) is a combination of hardware, software, infrastructure, data, procedures and trained personnel. With each of the components, we can bind specific risks that exist as a result of existence of their vulnerabilities. We talk about (Anderson 2010):

- Hardware vulnerabilities (natural catastrophes, physical deterioration),
- Software vulnerabilities (software misusage such as XSS, Buffer Overflow),
- Data vulnerability (obsolete data formats),
- Organizational vulnerabilities (mistakes and deficient procedures, user attitudes, information security culture),
- Human vulnerabilities (specific behaviour, limited perception etc.).

Several approaches exist for making predictions on vulnerability discoveries for individual IS components:

- Hardware: MTBF (Mean Time between Failures), MTTF (Mean Time to Failure)
- Software: VDM (Vulnerability Discovery Models) (Alhazmi et al. 2006)
- Human: NLP (Neuro-linguistic Programming), TA (transactional analysis) (Mann 2008)

Anticipating software vulnerability discoveries is not a completely new challenge. However, it became extremely important in the last decade with the development of web applications and technologies. Vulnerability Discovery Model (VDM) shall predict the time and the frequency of future discoveries. This information allows the software producers to acquire needed resources in order to fix defects on time.

The basic idea for VDM models came from Software Reliability Models (SRM). They are used for discovering software bugs. It turned out that the nature of the software vulnerabilities is different from bugs. That is why SRM models are not suitable for detecting vulnerabilities. There are several definitions of software vulnerabilities. In order to make clear distinction to the software bugs, we use the following one: *"Software vulnerability is an instance of a mistake in the specification, development, or configuration of software such that its execution can violate the security policy"* (Ozment 2007).

Several VDM models have been proposed in last years. According to their prediction approach, we separate them into two categories. *Effort-based models* are based on the number of product users. They are difficult to realize due to the lack of the needed data. Namely, the number of the product users is constantly changing and there are no accurate records about it (Woo et al. 2011). The second category is *Time-based models*. Among them Alhazmi-Malaiya Logistic model (AML) is the most accurate one (Alhazmi et al. 2006). It is based on a logistic function and on a quite simple assumption. In an early phase, when the product enters the market, it has a few users. Simultaneously, with increased popularity grows also the number of users. At the end of its life cycle, the number of users declines. According to the findings of the authors of AML model, vulnerability discoveries follow the same logistic function. See in Figure 1.

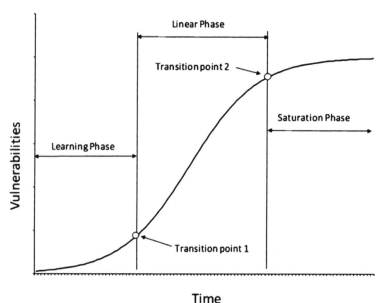

Figure 1 Vulnerability discoveries follow the logistic function

Proposed models only partly consider the factors that affect the discovery process. Besides the number of product users, we have to take into account the vulnerability management processes of software producers as well as the learning process of hackers (Frei et al. 2009).

Hackers (black and white ones) are more interested to discover vulnerabilities on the products, with the highest potential benefit for them. Generally, these are the most popular products on the market, which we can measure with the number of their users (Alhazmi et al. 2007). Publicly available data on discovered vulnerabilities show that the successful ideas quickly diffuse within the hackers' community and that we can find similar discoveries on many products. We can talk about the innovation diffusion phenomena. In this context, it is also important to mention, that one of the main sources from which the hackers learn, is patched program code (Arora et al. 2005).

The most dangerous are undiscovered and undisclosed vulnerabilities because software producers are not aware of them. There is simply no protection against attacks based on exploitation of such vulnerabilities. In order to mitigate the risk, the culture of responsible disclosure evolved. Individuals with positive intentions (ethical hackers) provide sensitive information to the software authors. They have a reasonable period of time (e.g. a week or a month) to eliminate product defects. Only when there is no response, ethical hackers disclose this sensitive information to the public. Unfortunately, the available time to patch the code significantly varies and is sometimes very short (Frei et al. 2009).

Frei et al. (Frei et al. 2009) introduced the model of existing vulnerability market. He identified all key agents and processes throughout the life cycle of vulnerability. Based on publicly available data he analysed the discovery process and identified the interests of particular groups. He describes the basic principles of the white market in details, while most of the properties of the black market stay unclear. Due to the nature of the black market and distrust between the threat agents, a detailed insight into the number of transactions is not possible. He concludes that black hackers generally do not help each other to discover vulnerabilities. Similarly, software producers carefully guard the details of their internal vulnerability handling processes and we do not know much about that.

The black market remains the least studied. Like other today's businesses, it operates on the Internet via freely accessible web pages. It works irregularly, often moves and is occasionally advertised. Participants on the black forums have to obey specific rules to ensure the smooth functioning of the black market. Radianti (Radianti 2010) notes that participants in the black market are mobile, and do not belong only to a single forum. This attitude increases their success in selling their knowledge about vulnerabilities. By using the system dynamics simulation model, Radianti examined the possibility of destruction of the black market on the Internet by using rigorous punishment. He concludes that penalties should be so high that prices on the black market would rise above the acceptable level for buyers (Radianti et al. 2010). Unclear remains typical behaviour of black market participants in relation to the white market. Do they sell only to the black market or do they occasionally participate also on the white market to earn additional money?

The existence of black and white market proves that the malicious threats exist. When a software producer launches a completely new product, it is unlikely that it would be attractive to attackers at once. Malicious threats do not exist at the very beginning and something has to give them a birth. We believe that some key factors exist, which have an impact on the process of creation of new malicious threats. Unfortunately, in the existing literature there are no models for predicting threats. Therefore, we place the following research questions:

RQ1: Which models exist for predicting people behaviour?
RQ2: Which data can be used to estimate the time, when the software product became attractive to the threat agents?

Answers to these research questions will help us develop the model for detecting malicious threats and hopefully to predict them in advance by using planned changes within the IS and its user environment.

3. Opportunities for making predictions about malicious threats

We make predictions on some existing facts or estimates. For predictions of malicious threats we need an appropriate definition of threat. In general, threat can be defined as a function of motivation, the expected impact for the attacker, his or her capability to carry out the attack, and the opportunities for the realization of an attack (Vidalis et al. 2005) (Eq. 2):

$$Threat = f(motiv,\ impact,\ capability,\ opportunity)\ (2)$$

The impact is directly related to the asset value, because IS assets are those targets within the IS, which are interesting to attackers and consequently they represent harm to the IS owner. When we combine the definition of threat with the one for security risk, we get the model on the Figure 2.

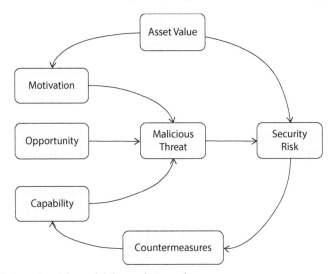

Figure 2 Security risk model for malicious threats

Malicious threat appears when all threat components are available. There is always a human behind the malicious threat. Therefore, we should somehow understand his or her behaviour. In case of a threat agent, we can speak about the misuse or abuse of information technology. On the field of IT/IS, several models have been developed to assess the acceptance and use of technology. Davis (Davis 1989) proposed the technology acceptance model (TAM) with the following key concepts:

- *Perceived ease of use (PEOU)*: degree to which a person believes that the system is easy to use,
- *Perceived usefulness (PU)*: degree to which a person believes that the system will be useful in performing his or her job,
- *Behavioural intention (BI)*: degree to which a person has formulated conscious plans to perform or not perform some specified future behaviour.

TAM is a flexible model. It has been extended several times and adapted into specific domains. Thorough observation of TAM concepts reveals similarities with the malicious threat components. PEOU can be related to the opportunities and PU to motivation.

Among other important acceptance models, we should also put out some other models (Oye et al. 2012): the theory of reasoned action (TRA), the motivational model (MM), the theory of planned behaviour (TPB) and the innovation diffusion theory (IDT). Venkatesh et al. (Venkatesh et al. 2003) reviewed the existing acceptance models and formulated the unified theory of acceptance and use of technology (UTAUT). This new model outperforms other existing acceptance models in predicting user behaviour. UTAUT model consists of the following constructs (causal relationships are depicted on Figure 3):

- *Performance expectancy (PE)*: degree to which an individual believes that using the system will help him or her to attain gains in job performance,
- *Effort expectancy (EE)*: degree of ease associated with the use of system,
- *Social influence (SI)*: degree to which an individual perceives that important others believe he or she should use the system,
- *Facilitating conditions (FC)*: degree to which an individual believes that an organizational and technical infrastructure exists to support use of the system.

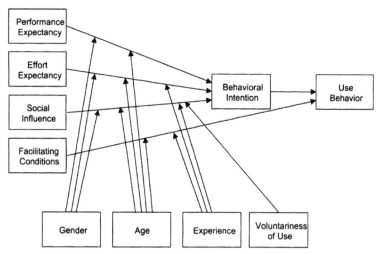

Figure 3 UTAUT model

We can find many researches using the UTAUT model in the area of eLearning systems, mobile services, process automation and some others (Oye et al. 2012). Up to our knowledge, no similar studies have been done in the security domain. Our idea is to adapt the UTAUT model with factors that are specific for attackers and instead of "usage" we will check the "misusage of technology". The expected result is the acceptance model, which will help us understand the mind-set of malicious threat agent on targeted system.

Another crucial building block upon which we can make predictions is the evidence of existing malicious threats. They leave trails behind their activities. Therefore, it is important to uncover the circumstances of the first occurrence of threat for the observed IS. A good approximation of the first appearance of malicious threat is the date of the first vulnerability discovery.

Thanks to some organizations (MITRE-CVE (MITRE n.d.), NIST-NVD (NIST n.d.)), which take care for publication of discovered vulnerabilities of most popular products on the market, such data exist. They are publicly available and will be used in our future studies. On Figure 4 the vulnerability discovery trail is represented for Wordpress product. We can see that the first discovery appeared in 2004 and some time before that malicious threat agent started activity. Consequently, the Wordpress became attractive for the attackers in that time.

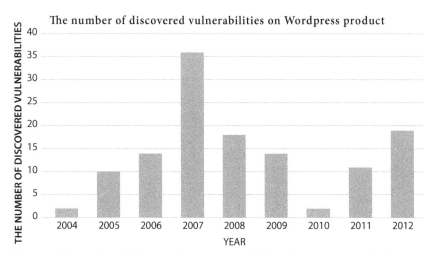

Figure 4 First vulnerability was discovered in 2004 and some time earlier threats.

4. Conclusion

Many studies have already pointed out the need to anticipate the discovery of vulnerabilities in software. However, the field of IT security is enormously intertwined with the human factor and we should pay attention on human vulnerabilities as well. Another important building block for security assessment are threats. The most complex threats for the information system are malicious threats. There are always people behind them. Therefore, we should understand the basic features about the attackers' mind-set and his or her behaviour. In this paper, we presented some ideas of how we could detect or predict the appearance of malicious threat. We concluded that the technology acceptance models could be useful to determine the key factors, which give birth to new malicious threats. In order to determine the real values of these key factors, we can help us with the databases of discovered vulnerabilities and other types of attacker' activity trails.

In future research we will focus on adaptation of UTAUT model for the purposes of better understanding the malicious attackers' behaviour. Another research goal is to analyze the existing data about some important software products on the market in order to determine the circumstances of some key factors at the time of first vulnerability discovery.

Acknowledgements

Work supported by Creative Core FISNM-3330–13-500033 'Simulations' project funded by the European Union, The European Regional Development Fund. The operation is carried out within the framework of the Operational Programme for Strengthening Regional Development Potentials for the period 2007–2013, Development Priority 1: Competitiveness and research excellence, Priority Guideline 1.1: Improving the competitive skills and research excellence.

List of References

Alhazmi, O. / Malaiya, Y.: "Prediction capabilities of vulnerability discovery models". In *Proceedings of the 17th International Symposium on Software Reliability Engineering"*, 2006, pp. 343–352.

Alhazmi, O.H. / Malaiya, Y.K. / Ray, I.: "Measuring, analyzing and predicting security vulnerabilities in software systems". *Computers & Security*, 2007, 26(3), pp. 219–228.

Anderson, R.J. : *Security Engineering. A Guide to Building Dependable Distributed Systems*. Wiley 2010.

Arora, A. / Telang, R.: "Economics of software vulnerability disclosure". *IEEE Security and Privacy Magazine*, 2005, 3(1), pp. 20–25.

Davis, F.D.: "Perceived Usefulness , Perceived Ease Of Use , And User Acceptance". *MIS Quarterly*, 1989, 13, pp. 319–340.

Frei, S. / Schatzmann, D. / Plattner, B. / Trammell, B.: "Modelling the Security Ecosystem – The Dynamics of (In) Security". In *Workshop on the Economics of Information Security (WEIS)*, 2009.

Mann, I. : *Hacking the Human: Social Engineering Techniques and Security Countermeasures*, Gower 2008.

MITRE: Common Vulnerabilities and Exposures, retrieved 10.12.2013 from http://cve.mitre.org/.

NIST: National Vulnerability Database, retrieved 10.12.2013 from http://nvd.nist.gov/.

Oye, N.D. / A.Iahad, N. / Ab.Rahim, N.: "The history of UTAUT model and its impact on ICT acceptance and usage by academicians". *Education and Information Technologies,* 2012.

Ozment, A.: "Vulnerability discovery & software security". (doctoral thesis) 2007.

Radianti, J.: "A Study of a Social Behaviour inside the Online Black Markets". *Fourth International Conference on Emerging Security Information, Systems and Technologies*, 2010, pp. 189–194.

Radianti, J. / Rich, E.: "Refinement of Supply and Demand Model for Vulnerability Black Market". In *2010 International System Dynamics Conference Seoul*, 2010.

Venkatesh, V. / Morris, M.D. / Davis, B.D. / Davis, F.D.: "User acceptance of information technology: Toward a unified view". *MIS quarterly*, 2003, 27(3), pp. 425–478.

Vidalis, S. / Jones, A.: "Analyzing Threat Agents & Their Attributes". In *Proceedings of the 5th European Conference on Information warfare and Security*, 2005, pp. 1–15.

Andrej Dobrovoljc

Woo, S.W. / Joh, H. / Alhazmi, O. / Malaiya, Y.: "Modeling vulnerability discovery process in Apache and IIS HTTP servers". *Computers & Security*, 2011, 30(1), pp. 50–62.

Blaž Rodič, Dejan Fortuna
Faculty of Information Studies, Novo mesto, Slovenia

Awareness of privacy issues in social networks

Abstract: The paper presents the results of a study in which we assessed how Facebook users in Slovenia perceived their privacy in social networks vs. in real life dependant of their age. We postulated a research question "To what extent are the users of Facebook aware of the privacy related issues?" and a hypothesis "Understanding of privacy on Facebook is different from the real world as Facebook users are willing to share more personal data online than in the real world." We carried out a quantitative study among younger Facebook users, and the results suggest that users have a limited awareness of the threats privacy in social networks, and that they assign less importance to privacy in social networks than in the real world as they are likely to share more personal information in social networks than on the street.

Keywords: online social networks, privacy, Facebook, personal data privacy policy

1. Introduction

The Internet has brought new threats to the security of personal data and privacy of users of online services. In the field of personal data and privacy security the online social networks present a distinct challenge, both in terms of security policy of such networks and in the users' attitude to their privacy.

In Slovenia in year 2010, 60 % of respondents had a profile in at least one social network. Younger users dominate social networks, since 75 % of all pupils or students use at least one social network (Jerman Kuželički/ Lebar/Vehovar 2011).

Our empirical observation is that the users of social networks feel less exposed in making virtual contacts than in real life, and willing to share a lot of personal information with the wide circle of "friends". The reason is, in our opinion, the virtual nature of social networks, where individuals have a different attitude towards other people than in real life, and trust has a different meaning. This is primarily reflected in the size of the user's "network of friends" which is much higher than in real life. The difference is also that real life friendships are defined differently than in social networks. (Gross/Acquisti 2005)

If we look at the use of social networking sites in terms of time spent, the most popular network is Facebook. In mid-March 2011, 627,360 people in Slovenia have used Facebook, which is 51 % of those who have ever used the Internet, and 37 % of the Slovenian population between 10 and 74 years of age. Most users are aged between 25 and 34 years, followed by the age group of 18 to 24 years (Raba interneta v Sloveniji 2011).

Jones and Hiram Soltren (2005) state that privacy on Facebook is jeopardized by three key factors: (1) users reveal too much personal information; (2) Facebook does not take adequate measures to protect personal privacy and (3) third parties, mainly advertising companies are actively looking for information about the end user. Only when these three factors are put together, the whole problem of privacy on Facebook exists. "According to the report Privacy and Human Rights 1999, privacy is jeopardized by three major trends: globalization (removing geographical restrictions on the flow of data), convergence of technologies (these are mutually increasingly interoperable), and multi-media (data in some form can change quickly)" (Kovačič 2003).

2. Methodology

In our study we observed how users perceive their privacy in social networks compared to its perception in the real world and how well they know the issues of privacy and security measures in social networks. Due to the prevalence of Facebook, we have focused our research on the users of this online social network.

We have asked the following research question: "To what extent are the users of Facebook aware of the privacy related issues?"

At the same time, we postulated the following hypothesis: "Understanding of privacy on Facebook is different from the real world as Facebook users are willing to share more personal data online than in the real world."

In the case of social networks, it seems that the word "privacy" is really losing its meaning. Many people are reluctant to share information such as their hobbies and birth date with casual acquaintances on the street. But it seems that if the same person were to add us as a friend on Facebook, reluctance would fade. This is in our opinion due to the physical separation from "friends" and events in the virtual world of online social networks. Because of this separation individuals have a stronger sense of security in their virtual interactions than in real life interaction.

Our research sample included Facebook users within our personal social network and in our "friends" social networks. Sample was further limited by age and included only users between 16 and 25 years of age. This limit was imposed to limit the relevancy of results to the age group, which dominates the social networks (Raba interneta v Sloveniji 2011). Because of sample size (201 respondents) and the geographical dispersion of the sample we have chosen online survey as our research tool. We used the tool 1KA, which is available online at https://www.1ka.si/. The tool is free for use and is developed in the context of social informatics study program at the Faculty of Social Sciences in the University in Ljubljana.

In order to determine how Facebook users perceive privacy in this network, we used a questionnaire, which consisted of 27 questions, of which the first three questions were demographic. We present the main findings of the research.

3. Results

Our survey was at least partially completed by 201 of 353 respondents (57 %), which is a good response for an online survey. The percentage of fully completed surveys was slightly lower, at 50 %. 61 % of respondents were male and 39 % were female, a significant difference with the demographic data for a previous nationwide research where 51 % of users were male and 49 % female (Raba interneta v Sloveniji 2013). Most of respondents have completed four years of secondary school (62 %), with 13 % followed by respondents with completed high school or Bologna first level study (Figure 1).

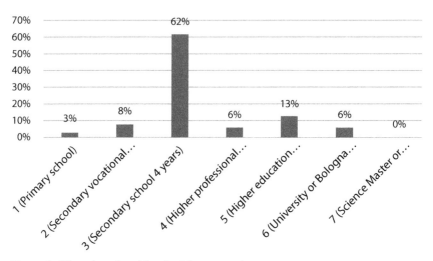

Figure 1: The educational level of the respondents

The majority of respondents (78 %) were "16 to 25 years" old and the next largest age group was "26 to 35 years" with 15 %. Respondents have been using Facebook for 1 to 7 years, with the average duration of 4.3 years (standard deviation was 1.12 years).

We were also interested which social networks the respondents also use in addition to Facebook. The largest number of respondents (34 responded that they do not use other social networking sites. Twitter was used by 30 % of respondents, followed by Netlog at 15 % and LinkedIn at 11 %. Other selected social networks were Instagram, Google+, Tumblr and Vine (respondents could choose several answers).

With the next set of questions we wanted to see how the users take care of their safety on Facebook by using some basic tools such as signing out and using a secure connection. The majority of respondents (85 %) which access their account via a public computer, always sign out, while many users, which use Facebook on their own PCs and mobile devices never sign out. 41 % of own PC users and 52 % of mobile device users do not sign out (Figure 2).

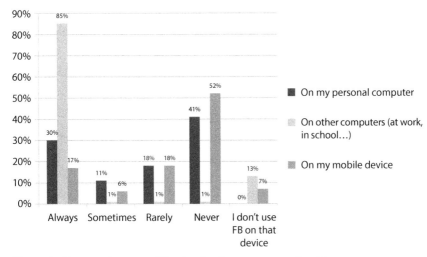

Figure 2: Do you sign out of Facebook after you stop using it?

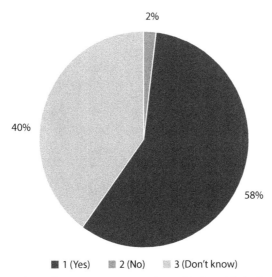

Figure 3: Do you have the option "Keep me logged in" enabled after the sign in?

In our survey 58 % of respondents choose the option "Keep me logged in" after they sign into Facebook. We have asked these 58 % whether they know that this option allows all the following users to access their Facebook account without a password, and 89 % of respondents replied that they are aware of that (Figure 3). This is somewhat surprising, since respondents are obviously aware of the danger, but choose to ignore it.

Next we asked users about the size of their networks, and how many people they know only on Facebook (Figure 4). The most common (21 %) is a networks with 201 to 300 friends, closely followed (20 %) by a network of 701 or more friends, and 18 % of networks have from 301 to 400 friends, and then (16 %) networks with 401 to 500 friends (Figure 4). According to the RIS, the average user in 2012 had 130 friends (Raba interneta v Sloveniji 2012).

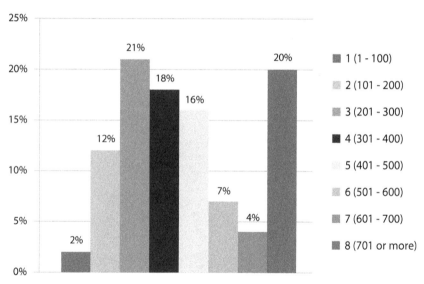

Figure 4: How many friends do you have on Facebook?

The next question also referred to the number of friends, but here we wanted to find out how many "friends" the users only met on Facebook. The result is quite surprising and may also worrying, as 18 % of users have 91 or more friends that they've never met outside of Facebook (Figure 5). However, 44 % of the users have only up to 10 Facebook-only "friends". Facebook has introduced the option to categorize "friends" in several groups according to what we want to share with them, which can be used to protect ones privacy. In our research, 78 % of the respondents were aware of this option. However, only one third of these 78 % use this option.

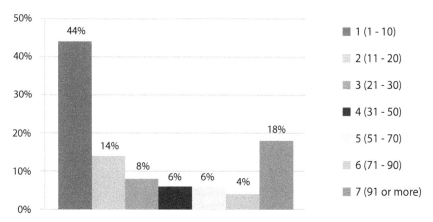

Figure 5: How many of your Facebook "friends" do you know only through Facebook?

We also asked the users whether they have read the Terms of Service and Data use/Privacy Policy, and were not surprised that more than half of the respondents have not read these documents at all, and only 6 % (likely the same group for both documents) read them in entirety (Figure 6).

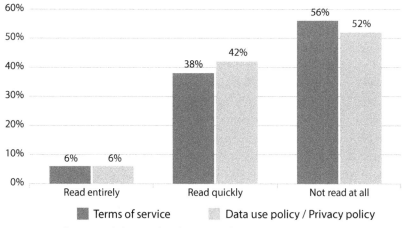

Figure 6: Did you read the Facebook Terms of service and Data use/Privacy policy?

However, most respondents (74 %) have at least changed the default Face-book privacy settings (Figure 7). The survey-included questions regarding details of the security settings, e.g. separate friend lists, but due to limited paper size in this publication we are unable to list all of them. Readers are welcome to inquire with authors regarding the full survey results.

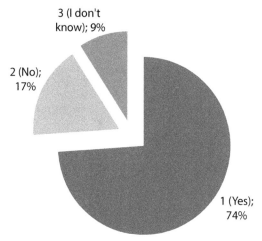

Figure 7: Have you changed the default privacy settings?

The terms of use state that the user must provide accurate personal in-formation when registering (Raba interneta v Sloveniji 2012). We asked respondents what personal information they added to their profile and whether the information is correct. The full list of categories included in the survey would make the graph hard to read; therefore only selected catego-ries are shown in Figure 8. We have inquired about the following: Name, Surname, Date of birth, Mobile number, Email address, Residence, Educa-tion, Marital status, Employment, Religion, Political persuasion, Hobbies. Basic personal information such as name was entered by 99 % of users, probably to be found and contacted by their real life acquaintances more easily. Many users also entered information about their birthday (82 %). Of these 82 %, 64 % have entered the entire birth date, while 36 % of users entered only the day and month of birth. Upon registration, we can also provide an e-mail address, which can be hidden from other users. 46 % of respondents entered their e-mail address but do not share it, while 50 %

also share their e-mail address with "friends". Other information that users share includes their place of residence (51 %), education (76 %), workplace (27 %), hobbies (25 %) and telephone number (13 %). Very few respondents have entered false information.

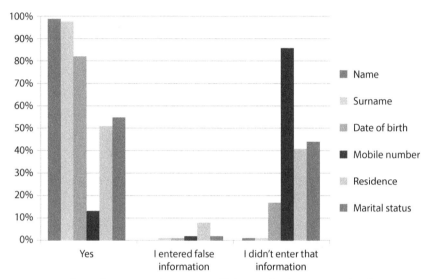

Figure 8: What information about yourself do you disclose on Facebook?

These results are in contrast with the respondent's willingness to share the same personal information on the street with a stranger or a casual acquaintance (Figure 9). From the answers we can conclude that they are not willing to share personal information with someone we do not know well. More than half are willing to share personal information in certain circumstances (sometimes). Basic personal information (name and surname) would never be shared by 11 % of respondents, which is significantly more than 1 % of respondents on Facebook, and an even greater percentage of respondents would never share their birth date (29 % compared with 18 % on Facebook) and phone numbers (only 5 % would always share their number in the street, compared with 13 % who share their phone number on Facebook). When it comes to sharing personal information it seems that people are willing to share a lot more online than in real life.

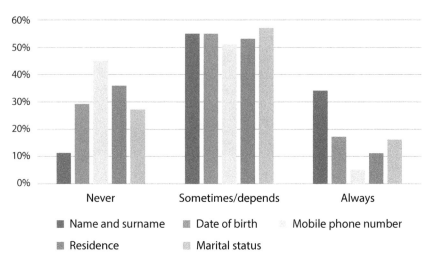

Figure 9: What personal information would you be willing to share on the street with a stranger or a casual acquaintance?

4. Discussion

In our study, we presented a research question and one hypothesis. Research question was: "To what extent are the users of Facebook aware of the privacy related issues?" We can reply that the users are to some extent aware of the problems related to privacy and are limiting access to their profile and posts, but many add complete strangers to their network of "friends". One statistic that has improved since 2008 is the changing of default privacy settings. In 2008 only 20 % of users changed the default privacy settings, compared to 75 % of the respondents in our survey. However, few people sign out of Facebook after use. More than half of the respondents did not read the terms and policies of registration, although they had to confirm that they did when registering.

Our hypothesis was: "Understanding of privacy on Facebook is different from the real world as Facebook users are willing to share more personal data online than in the real world." Although in our opinion it is easier to determine whether you can trust a person when talking with them live than in the virtual world, the perception of privacy has changed, not only in the virtual space, but also in real life. As stated by the founder of Facebook, privacy is no longer a social norm and everything is public, everything is to be shared (Kučić 2011). It is not surprising that according to the findings of our research young people are much more willing to share personal information with acquaintances and strangers on Facebook than in the street. The hypothesis can therefore be confirmed.

We can conclude that today's youth has a relaxed attitude towards privacy in social networks and are prepared to share their personal data and information about their private lives with casual acquaintances and strangers. Although this is a disturbing due to the potentials for abuse, there is also a bright side to this phenomenon: the world is becoming a global village, in which geographical restrictions have a declining influence in shaping of communities, and we can postulate a new hypothesis for the future research: in online social networks, young people socialize regardless of differences in race, nationality and religion.

List of References

Facebook: *Statement of rights and responsibilities*, https://www.facebook.com/legal/terms, retrieved: 21.5.2013.

Gross, Ralph/ Acquisti, Alessandro: *Information revelation and privacy in online social networks. Workshop on privacy in the electronic society*, http://privacy.cs.cmu.edu/dataprivacy/projects/facebook/facebook1.pdf, retrieved: 3.3.2013, 2005.

Jerman Kuželički, Ajda/ Lebar, Lea and Vehovar, Vasja: *Socialna omrežja 2011*, http://www.ris.org/db/13/12076/RIS%20poro%C4%8Dila/, 2011. Socialna_omrezja_2011/?&p1=276&p2=285&p3=1318, retrieved: 19.3.2013, 2011.

Jones, Harvey/ Hiram Soltren, Jose: *Facebook: Threats to privacy*, http://groups.csail.mit.edu/mac/classes/6.805/student-papers/fall05-papers/facebook.pdf, retrieved: 30. 4. 2013, 2005.

Kovačič, Matej: *Zasebnost na internetu*. Ljubljana: Mirovni inštitut, 2003.

Kučić, Lenart J.: "Počutim se kot nori okoljevarstvenik iz šestdesetih let". Delo – Sobotna priloga, 12. november 2011, pg. 18–19, 2011.

Raba interneta v Sloveniji, *Na Facebooku skoraj 630.000 prebivalcev Slovenije*, http://www.ris.org/index.php?fl=2&lact=1&bid=11980&parent=27, downloaded: 20. 3. 2013, 2011.

Raba interneta v Sloveniji: *Povprečen Facebook uporabnik ima 130 prijateljev*, http://www.ris.org/db/26/12323//Povprecen_Facebook_, 2012. uporabnik_ima_130_prijateljev/?q=prijateljifacebook&qdb=26&qso rt=0, retrieved: 19.7.2013.

Raba interneta v Sloveniji: *Na Facebooku skoraj 750.000 slovenskih uporabnikov,* http://www.ris.org/db/27/12535/Raziskave/Na_Facebooku_,2013. skoraj_750000_slovenskih_uporabnikov/?&p1=276&p2=285 &p3=1318, retrieved: 17.7.2013.

Domagoj Margan, Sanda Martinčić-Ipšić, Ana Meštrović
Department of Informatics, University of Rijeka
Radmile Matejčić 2, 51000 Rijeka, Croatia
{dmargan, smarti, amestrovic}@uniri.hr

Preliminary Report on the Structure of Croatian Linguistic Co-occurrence Networks

Abstract: In this article, we investigate the structure of Croatian linguistic co-occurrence networks. We examine the change of network structure properties by systematically varying the co-occurrence window sizes, the corpus sizes and removing stop words. In a co-occurrence window of size n we establish a link between the current word and $n - 1$ subsequent words. The results point out that the increase of the co-occurrence window size is followed by a decrease in diameter, average path shortening and expectedly condensing the average clustering coefficient. The same can be noticed for the removal of the stop words. Finally, since the size of texts is reflected in the network properties, our results suggest that the corpus influence can be reduced by increasing the co-occurrence window size.

Keywords: complex networks, linguistic co-occurrence networks, Croatian corpus, stop words

1. Introduction

The complex networks sub-discipline tasked with the analysis of language has been recently associated with the term of linguistic's network analysis. Text can be represented as a complex network of linked words: each individual word is a node and interactions amongst words are links. The interactions can be derived at different levels: structure, semantics, dependencies, etc. Commonly they rise from a simple criterion such as co-occurrence of two words within a sentence, or text.

The pioneering construction of linguistic networks was when Ferrer i Cancho (2001) showed that the co-occurrence network from the British National Corpus has a small average path length, a high clustering coefficient, and a two-regime power law degree distribution; the network exhibits small-world and scale-free properties. Drogotsev (2001) used complex networks to study language as a self-organizing network of interacting words. The co-occurrence networks were constructed by linking two neighbouring words within a sentence. Masucci (2006) investigated the network topology of Orwell's '1984' focusing on the local properties: nearest neighbours and the clustering coefficient by linking the neighbouring words. Pardo (2006) used the complex network's clustering coefficient as the measure of text summarization performance. The original and summarized texts were preprocessed with stop words' removal and lemmatization. For the network construction reversed window orientation was used, which caused the word to be connected to the previous words with forwarding links' directions. Caldiera (2006) examined the structure of the texts of individual authors. After stop word elimination and lemmatization each sentence was added to the network as a clique[1]. Biemann (2012) compared networks where two neighbouring words were linked with networks where all the words co-occurring in the sentence were linked. From the network properties they derived a quantifiable measure of generative language (n-gram artificial language) regarding the semantics of natural language. Borge-Holthoefer (2010) produced a methodological and formal overview of complex networks from the language research perspective. Liu and Cong (2013) used complex network parameters for the classification (hierarchical clustering) of 14 languages, where Croatian was amongst 12 Slavic.

In this paper we construct the linguistic co-occurrence networks from Croatian texts. We examine the change of a network's structure properties by systematically varying the co-occurrence window sizes, the corpus sizes and stopwords' removal. In a co-occurrence window of size n we establish a link between the current word and $n - 1$ subsequent words.

In Section 2 we define network properties needed to accurately analyse small-world and scale-free characteristics of co-occurrence networks, such as diameter, average path length and average clustering coefficient. In Section 3 we present the construction of 30 co-occurrence networks. The network measurements are in Section 4. In the final Section, we elaborate on the obtained results and make conclusions regarding future work.

---

1   A clique in an undirected network is a subset of its nodes such that every two nodes in the subset are linked.

2. The network structure analysis

In the network N is the number of nodes and K is the number of links. In weighted networks every link connecting two nodes has an associated weight $w \in R_0^+$. The co-occurrence window m_n of size n is defined as n subsequent words from a text. The number of network components is denoted ω.

For every two connected nodes i and j the number of links lying on the shortest path between them is denoted as d_{ij}, therefore the average distance of a node i from all other nodes is:

$$d_i = \frac{\sum_j d_{ij}}{N}.$$

And the average path length between every two nodes i,j is:

$$L = \sum_{i,j} \frac{d_{ij}}{N(N-1)}.$$

The maximum distance results in the network diameter:

$$D = \max_i d_i.$$

For weighted networks the clustering coefficient of a node i is defined as the geometric average of the subgraph link weights:

$$c_i = \frac{1}{k_i(k_i-1)} \sum_{i,j} (\hat{w}_{ij} \hat{w}_{ik} \hat{w}_{jk})^{\frac{1}{3}},$$

where the link weights $\hat{w}_{ij}$ are normalized by the maximum weight in the network $\hat{w}_{ij} = \hat{w}_{ij}/\max(w)$. The value of c_i is assigned to 0 if $k_i < 2$.

The average clustering of a network is defined as the average value of the clustering coefficients of all nodes in a network:

$$C = \frac{1}{N} \sum_i c_i.$$

If $\omega > 1$, C is computed for the largest network component.

An important property of complex networks is degree distribution. For many real networks this distribution follows power law, which is defined as: $P(k) \sim k^{-\alpha}$.

3. Network construction

3.1 Data

For the construction and analysis of co-occurrence networks, we used a corpus of literature, containing 10 books written in or translated into the Croatian language. For the experiments we divided the corpus into three parts: C1 – one book, C2 – four books and C3 – ten books, where C1 ⊆ C2 ⊆ C3, as shown in Table 1.

Stop words are a list of the most common, short function words which do not carry strong semantic properties, but are needed for the syntax of language (pronouns, prepositions, conjunctions, abbreviations, interjections,...). The Croatian stop words list contains 2,923 words in their inflected forms. Examples of stop words are: 'is', 'but', 'and', 'which', 'on', 'any', 'some'.

Table 1: The statistics for the corpus of 10 books

Corpus part	C1	C2	C3
# of words	28671	252328	895547
# of unique words	9159	40221	91018
# of stop words	371	588	629

3.2 The construction of co-occurrence networks

We constructed 30 different co-occurrence networks, weighted and directed, from the corpus in Table 1. Words are nodes, and they are linked if they are in the same sentence according to the size of the co-occurrence window. The co-occurrence window m_n of size n is defined as a set of n subsequent words from a text. Within a window the links are established between the first word and $n - 1$ subsequent words. During the construction we considered the sentence boundary as the window boundary too. Three steps in the network construction for a sentence of 5 words, and the co-occurrence window size $n = 2..5$ is shown in Figure 1.

The weight of the link between two nodes is proportional to the overall co-occurrence frequencies of the corresponding words within a co-occurrence window. For all three parts of the corpus C1, C2, C3, we examined the properties of co-occurrence networks constructed with various m_n, $n = 2, 3, 4, 5, 6$. Besides 5 window sizes for co-occurrence networks, we also differentiate upon the criterion of the inclusion or exclusion of stopwords.

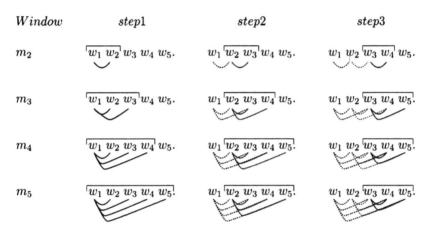

Figure 1: An illustration of 3 steps in a network construction with a co-occurrence window m_n of sizes $n = 2..5$. $w_1 \ldots w_5$ are words within a sentence.

Network construction and analysis was implemented with the Python programming language using the NetworkX software package developed for the creation, manipulation, and study of the structure, dynamics, and functions of complex networks (Hagberg 2008). Numerical analysis and visualization of power law distributions was made with the 'powerlaw' software package for the Python programming language (Alstott 2014).

4. Results

Table 2: Networks constructed from C1. Measures noted with the *sw* subscript are results with stop words included.

	m_2	m_3	m_4	m_5	m_6
N_{sw}	9530	9530	9530	9530	9530
N	9159	9159	9159	9159	9159

	m_2	m_3	m_4	m_5	m_6
K_{sw}	22305	43894	64161	83192	101104
K	14627	28494	41472	53596	64840
L_{sw}	3.59	2.92	2.70	2.55	2.45
L	6.42	4.73	4.12	3.79	3.58
D_{sw}	16	9	7	6	6
D	26	15	11	10	8
C_{sw}	0.15	0.55	0.63	0.66	0.68
C	0.01	0.47	0.56	0.60	0.64
ω_{sw}	5	5	5	5	5
ω	15	15	15	15	15

The comparisons of the properties for networks differing in the co-occurrence window size are shown in Tables 2, 3 and 4. Clearly, the results show that the networks constructed with larger co-occurrence window emphasize small-world properties. More precisely, the values of the average path length and network diameter decrease proportionally to the increase of co-occurrence window size. Likewise, the average clustering coefficient becomes larger in accordance with the increment of m_n.

Table 3: Networks constructed from C2. Measures noted with the *sw* subscript are results with stop words included.

	m_2	m_3	m_4	m_5	m_6
N_{sw}	40809	40809	40809	40809	40809
N	40221	40221	40221	40221	40221
K_{sw}	156857	307633	445812	572463	688484
K	108449	207437	296233	375535	446547
L_{sw}	3.25	2.81	2.64	2.52	2.43
L	4.69	3.86	3.54	3.35	3.23

	m_2	m_3	m_4	m_5	m_6
D_{sw}	18	12	8	7	6
D	24	14	11	9	9
C_{sw}	0.25	0.58	0.65	0.68	0.70
C	0.02	0.43	0.52	0.56	0.59
ω_{sw}	9	9	9	9	9
ω	33	33	33	33	33

Table 4: Networks constructed from C3. Measures noted with the *sw* subscript are results with stop words included.

	m_2	m_3	m_4	m_5	m_6
N_{sw}	91647	91647	91647	91647	91647
N	91018	91018	91018	91018	91018
K_{sw}	464029	911277	1315888	1680848	2009187
K	360653	684008	963078	1202869	1409599
L_{sw}	3.10	2.74	2.58	2.47	2.38
L	4.17	3.55	3.30	3.16	3.08
D_{sw}	23	13	9	7	7
D	34	19	14	11	9
C_{sw}	0.32	0.61	0.67	0.69	0.71
C	0.03	0.42	0.51	0.55	0.58
ω_{sw}	22	22	22	22	22
ω	64	64	64	64	64

In Tables 2, 3 and 4 we also compare the characteristics of networks with the removal of the stop words. In addition to the proportional strengthening of small-world properties with the increase of m_n, the same phenomenon appears with the inclusion of stop words in the process of building the network. All of the networks show smaller network distance measures and greater clustering coefficient with the stop words included.

Furthermore, stop words have an impact on the average clustering coefficient in a way that increasing the corpus size with the stop words included will result in a higher clustering coefficient, while increasing the corpus size with the stop words excluded will result in a lower clustering coefficient (Figure 2). This may be explained by the high impact of stop words as the main hubs. Table 5 shows that stop words are much stronger hubs than other hubs, which we gain with the exclusion of stop words.

Table 5: Top ten hubs in networks constructed from C3.

SW included				SW excluded			
m_2		m_8		m_2		m_8	
i (and)	29762	i (and)	67890	kad (when)	4260	kad (when)	14921
je (is)	13924	je (is)	53484	rekao (said)	2036	rekao (said)	5755
u (in)	13116	se (self)	42563	sad (now)	1494	jedan (one)	5142
se (self)	11033	u (in)	41188	reče (said)	1319	sad (now)	5062
na (on)	9084	da (yes, that)	35632	jedan (one)	1318	ljudi (people)	4836
da (yes)	8103	na (on)	29417	ima (has)	1281	dana (day)	4679
a (but)	6637	su (are)	22366	ljudi (people)	1264	ima (has)	4406
kao (as)	5452	a (but)	21919	dobro (good)	1119	reče (said)	4178
od (from)	4773	kao (as)	18141	dana (day)	998	dobro (good)	3964
za (for)	4708	ne (no)	16211	reći (say)	968	čovjek (human)	3496

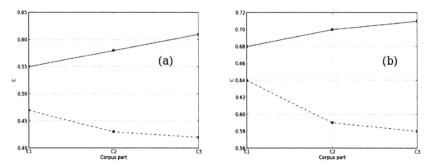

Figure 2: The impact of stop words on the average clustering coefficient in accordance with the various sizes of the corpus parts. C_{sw} (from networks constructed with stop words included) is represented by solid lines, while the C (from networks constructed with stopwords excluded) is represented by dashed lines. (a) m_3 networks, (b) m_6 networks.

Numerical results of power law distribution analysis indicate the presence of the power law distribution. The visualization of power law distribution for 4 networks created from C3 is shown in Figure 3. We found that networks constructed with included stop words generally represent a good power law fit starting from the optimal x_{min}. The numeric values of α for the power law distributions shown in Figure 2 are respectively: 2.167, 2.172, 2.339, 2.040. The networks with stop words included have a better power law fit.

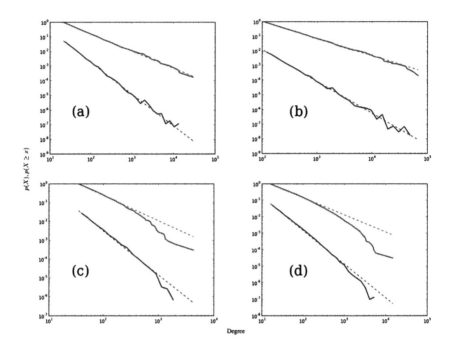

Figure 3: Comparison of plots. Probability density function ($p(X)$, lower line) and complementary cumulative distribution function ($p(X \geq x)$, upper line) of node degrees from networks constructed from C3: (a) m_2, stopwords included, (b) m_6, stop words included, (c) m_2, stop words excluded, (d) m_6, stop words excluded.

5. Conclusion

In this work we have presented multiple metrics of complex networks constructed as co-occurrence networks from the Croatian language. Since, the sensitivity of the linguistic network parameters to the corpus size and stop words (Caldeira 2006, Choudhury 2010) is a known problem in the construction of linguistic networks, we analysed the Croatian co-occurrence network. We presented the results of 30 networks constructed with the aim to examine variations among: corpus size, stop word removal and the size of the co-occurrence window.

The results in Tables 2, 3, 4, are pointing that the increase of the co-occurrence window size is followed by the diameter D decrease, average path L shortening and expectedly condensing the average clustering coefficient C. It is worth noticing, that the increased window size contributed to the results the same as the increase of the used quantity of texts did, suggesting emphasized small-world properties. The larger size of co-occurrence window plays a key role in the strengthening of properties of the small-world networks. This observation should be considered in detail in the prospect work.

Furthermore, the inclusion of stop words in the process of network construction causes the same effect. It is evident from Table 5 that stop words, although they have no strong semantic properties, act as hubs which can be cumbersome for semantic text analysis.

The inclusion of stop words in co-occurrence networks seems to contribute to the benefit of power law distribution, regardless of the co-occurrence window size. We point out the varying behaviour of the clustering coefficient (dynamics) by increasing the corpus size. According to our results, it depends on the presence of stop words in the corpus: increasing the corpus size with stop words included, increases the value of C, while increasing the corpus size with the stop words excluded, decreases the value of C.

Finally, since the size of texts is reflected in the network properties, our results suggest that the influence of the corpus can be reduced by increasing the co-occurrence window size. This paper is a preliminary study of the Croatian linguistic network, and more detailed research should be performed in the future. Firstly, the results should be tested on a larger corpus and power law and scale free properties proven. Additionally, the research towards extracting network semantics is a new and thrilling branch of our pursuit.

List of references

Alstott, Jeff / Bullmore, Ed / Plenz Dietmar: "powerlaw: a Python package for analysis of heavy-tailed distributions". *PloS one* 9(4) 2014, retrieved preprint 1.6.2013, from arXiv:1305.0215

Biemann, Chris / Roos, Stefanie / Weihe, Karsten: "Quantifying semantics using complex network analysis". In: Kay , Martin / Boited , Christian (eds.): *Proceedings of the 24th International Conference on Computational Linguistics. Tehnical papers*. The COLING 2012 Organizing Committe: Bombay 2012, pp 263–278.

Borge-Holthoefer, Javier / Arenas, Alex: "Semantic networks: structure and dynamics". *Entropy* 12(5) 2010, pp. 1264–1302.

Caldeira, Silvia *et al.*: "The network of concepts in written texts". *The European Physical Journal B – Condensed Matter and Complex Systems* 49(4) 2006, pp. 523–529.

Choudhury, Monojit / Chatterjee, Diptesh / Mukherjee, Animesh: "Global topology of word co-occurrence networks: Beyond the two-regime power-law". In: Huang Chu-Ren / Jurafski Dan (eds.): *Proceedings of the 23rd International Conference on Computational Linguistics. Posters.* The COLING 2010 Organizing Committe: Beijing 2010, pp. 162–170.

Dorogovtsev, Sergey / Mendes, José Fernando: "Language as an evolving word web". *Proceedings of the Royal Society of London B* 268(1485) 2001, pp. 2603–2606.

Ferrer i Cancho, Ramon / Solé, Richard: "The small world of human language". *Proceedings of the Royal Society of London B* 268(1482) 2001, pp. 2261–2265.

Hagberg, Aric A. / Schult, Daniel A. / Swart, Pieter J.: "Exploring network structure, dynamics, and function using NetworkX". In: Varoquax, Gael / Vaught, Travis / Millman, Jarrod (eds.): *Proceedings of the 7th Python in Science Conference.* The SciPy 2008 Organizing Committe: Pasadena 2008, pp. 11–15.

Liu, HaiTao / Cong, Jin: "Language clustering with word co-occurrence networks based on parallel texts". *Chinese Science Bulletin* 58(10) 2013, pp. 1139–1144.

Masucci, Paolo / Rodgers, Geoff: "Network properties of written human language". *Physical Review E* 74(2) 2006, retrieved 10.10.2012, from DOI 10.1103/PhysRevE.74.026102.

Pardo, Thiago Alexandre Salgueiro *et al.*: "Using complex networks for language processing: The case of summary evaluation". In: *Proceedings of the International Conference on Communications, Circuits and Systems.* IEEE Press: Guilin 2006, pp. 2678–2682.

Lucia Načinović Prskalo, Sanda Martinčić-Ipšić
Department of Informatics,University of Rijeka

Prosodic Modelling for Croatian Speech Synthesis

Abstract: In order to include prosody into text to speech systems (TTS), prosody knowledge needs to be acquired, represented and incorporated. Two main features of prosody important for modelling prosody for TTS systems are duration and F0 contour. There are various approaches to modelling those features and they can be categorized into three main groups: rule based, statistical and minimalistic. Some of the best known approaches to duration acquiring are Klatt's model, classification and regression trees and neural networks and to F0 modelling TOBI, Fujisaki and Tilt. A procedure for automatic intonation event detection on Croatian texts based on the Tilt model was evaluated in terms of Root Mean Square Error values for generated F0 contours.

Keywords: prosody modelling, speech synthesis, TTS, duration models, F0 contour models, prosodic characteristics of Croatian

1 Introduction

The main task of speech synthesis is the generation of voice signal understandable to listener from the text input. This implies that the synthesized speech should sound natural, and that it should own prosodic characteristics of natural human speech. Language conveys a wide range of information about the duration, intonation, emphasis, grouping words into phrases, voice quality, rhythm, etc., and these features are collectively referred to as – prosody. Prosody plays a great role in intelligibility, and especially in the naturalness of synthesized speech.

The ability of humans of using the prosody knowledge is naturally acquired but difficult to articulate. For synthesizing speech from a text by a machine this prosody knowledge needs to be acquired, represented and incorporated into speech synthesis procedures. Therefore prediction of the prosodic patterns directly from a text is not an easy task (Huang 2001). However, for this purpose, there are different models and algorithms that attempt to predict prosodic elements from texts. These models vary from models based on a set of rules to data driven models, such as classification and regression trees (CARTS) (Dusterhoff 1999) and Hidden Markov models (Taylor 2000). Besides the mentioned models that tend to fall into one of the basic categories, there are models that use additional methodology for example JEMA: Joint feature extraction and modelling (Rojc 2005) or combine rule-based approach with data driven approach (Aylett 2004).

This paper discusses the component of prosodic analysis in TTS systems. A procedure for automatic intonation event detection on Croatian texts is evaluated with Root Mean Square Error values for generated F0 contours using Tilt.

In the second section basic concepts of prosody in TTS systems are described. In the third section rule based, statistical and minimalistic approaches to prosody acquiring are outlined. Duration models are presented in the fourth section and F0 contour models in the fifth section. In the sixth section basic prosodic characteristics of Croatian and in the seventh related work for languages cognate to Croatian are outlined. A procedure for automatic intonation event detection for Croatian speech synthesis is presented in the eighth section. The paper concludes with our plans for future work for prosody modelling for Croatian TTS.

2 Prosody in TTS – basic concepts and definitions

Prosody is a complex combination of phonetic factors, which has a task to express attitude, assumptions and draw attention as a parallel channel of communication in our daily speech (Huang 2001).

Semantic content that is transmitted via voice or text message is also called denotation, and emotional aspects and the effects of intent that the speaker wishes to convey are a part of the message that is called connotation. Prosody plays an important role in the transmission of denotation, and a major role in the transmission of connotations (speaker's attitude toward the message, toward the listener and toward the overall communication event) (Huang 2001).

Prosody represents the acoustic properties of speech that transmit information, which is not conveyed by the word meaning such as emotions, discourse features, syntax (Fordyce 1998).

Two most important prosodic features that affect the quality of the synthesized speech are considered to be duration and F0 contour.

Duration refers to the duration of all speech particles: paragraph, sentence, intonation unit, speech word, syllables and phonemes. However, for TTS the duration of phonetic segments rather than the duration of words and syllables is used (van Santen 1997) (van Santen 1994). One of the reasons for this is that the pause (boundary) between segments, which is one of the most important prosodic features, can be relatively easy to determine automatically. Research regarding the duration on the level of syllables and phonemes were mostly focused on the duration of syllables in read speech (Kato 1998) (Stergar 2010). It has been shown that the duration of vowels depends on many factors, some of which include the articulatory context (phonemes before and after vowels), accent (both word accent and sentence accent) and position (the position of syllables in a word and speech unit).

The fundamental frequency (F0 contour) is determined by many factors such as segmental factors (micro intonation), patterns of stress, melody, rhythm, gender, attitude, and physical and emotional state of the speaker. Two main approaches to intonation acquiring are phonological models and phonetic (parameter based) models.

3 Basic approaches to prosody acquiring

Three main approaches to prosody acquiring have been distinguished so far: rule based approach, statistical approach and minimalistic approach.

3.1 Rule based approach

Rule based approach of implementing prosody into the synthesized speech uses written rules to predict prosodic characteristics from text. One of the best-known rule based approaches for the duration modelling is Klatt's MTalk system (Allen 1987). For F0 contour modelling the best-known rule based model is Pierrehumbert's system (Pierrehumbert 1981) in which the contour is described as a series of target values, which are connected together by transition rules. The target values are expressed as locations within the current pitch range. Which syllables within the phrase are assigned a target depends on the stress pattern. For example, in a declarative neutral intonation, all pitch accents are high (H), when the phrase is terminal, the phrase final tones are low-low (L-L) and if it is nonterminal, they are low-high (L-H).

3.2 Statistical approach

Statistical models are trained on labelled data. Hand-labelled prosodic features are used for parameter estimation. Parameters represent the probability of prosodic events in the context of different linguistic features. Model is used to predict the most likely prosodic labels on any input text.

One of the methods used in statistical approaches are decision-trees (CART – classification and regression trees) (Hirschberg 1995) (Ross 1996) (Ostendorf 1994). A list of possible features must be determined, and the system automatically selects features that have the greatest ability of prediction. Hidden Markov Models (HMMs) is another method that can be used to predict prosodic events. In (Taylor 2000) HMMs are used to predict phrase boundaries, and the model is trained on the information about the type of word and proceeding anticipated border. This approach requires a large amount of data for model training.

3.3 Minimalistic approach

In minimalistic approach, large natural language corpuses are used to train prosodic models, and as a source of units needed in the concatenation synthesis. There are several instances of units (most often diphones) with different characteristics in different phonetic and prosodic environments. One of the first systems that used unit selection approach in speech synthesis was CHATR: a generic speech synthesis system (Taylor 1994).

4 Approaches to duration modelling

As mentioned before, one of the two most important prosodic features in speech synthesis is duration. There are different approaches of duration modelling and some of them are described in this chapter.

4.1 Klatt's duration model

This model was developed in the 70ies and 80ies of the 20th century and is an integral part of a MITalk formant speech synthesizer (Allen 1987).

It is composed of sequential rules that include phonetic environment features, accents, shortening and lengthening of syllables at certain positions etc. Basic assumption in Klatt's model is that each segment has its inherent duration; each rule increases or decreases the duration of the segment for a certain percentage, and the duration of each segment cannot be decreased beyond minimal length.

4.2 CARTs

Some of the features that can be included in the duration modelling with classification and regression trees are phoneme identity, identity of phoneme to the left, identity of phoneme to the right etc. There are different programs for CARTS training and one of them is for example Wagon procedure in the Festival Speech Synthesis Systems (available at: http://www.cstr.ed.ac.uk/projects/festival/) .

4.3 Neural networks

Neural networks can be used in duration modelling (Campbell 1992). The model first predicts the duration of the syllable and then complements it with the phoneme duration. For each syllable vector, which consists of information about the number of the phonemes in the syllable, accent, part of speech tag etc. is calculated.

5 Approaches to F0 modelling

Phonological approaches to prosodic analysis of speech use a set of abstract phonological categories (tone, breaks etc.) to describe F0 contour and each category has its own linguistic function. An example of this approach is ToBI intonation model (Silverman 1992). Parameter based approaches attempt to describe F0 contour using a set of continuous parameters. Such approaches are, for example, Tilt intonation model (Taylor 2000) and Fujisaki model (Fujisaki 2005).

5.1 ToBI

ToBI (Tones and Break Indices) (Silverman 1992) takes a linguistic or phonological approach specifying a small set of discrete labels, which identify the intonational space of accents and tones. It is used for transcribing accents and phrasing (grouping of words). ToBI differs two pitch accents: H* or L* and four main boundary tones L-L%, L-H%, H-H%, H-L%. One pitch accent is associated to each accented word and one boundary tone is associated to the end of each prosodic phrase.

5.2 Fujisaki

Fujisaki model (Fujisaki 2005) describes F0 contour as a superposition of two contributions: a phrase component and an accent component. The phrase component models the baseline component and the accent component models micro prosodic variations. F0 contour is generated as a result of the superposition of the outputs of two second order linear filters with a base frequency value. The second order linear filters generate the phrase and accent components. The base frequency is the minimum frequency value of the speaker.

5.3 Tilt

Tilt is a phonetic model of intonation that represents intonation as a sequence of continuously parameterized events (pitch accents or boundary tones) (Taylor 2000). These parameters are called tilt parameters, determined directly from F0 contour. Basic units of a Tilt model are intonation events – the linguistically relevant parts of the F0 contour.

Parameters important for events detection are rise amplitude (Hz), rise duration (seconds), fall amplitude (Hz), fall duration (seconds), position (seconds) and F0 height (Hz). Those parameters can be transformed into Tilt parameters:

- Tilt-amplitude (Hz): the sum of the magnitudes of the rise and fall amplitudes:

$$tilt_{amp} = \frac{|A_{rise}| - |A_{fall}|}{|A_{rise}| + |A_{fall}|}$$

- Tilt-duration (seconds): the sum of the rise and fall durations:

$$tilt_{dur} = \frac{|D_{rise}| - |D_{fall}|}{|D_{rise}| + |D_{fall}|}$$

- Tilt: a dimensionless number which expresses the overall shape of the event, independent of its amplitude or duration:

$$tilt = \frac{|A_{rise}| - |A_{fall}|}{2|A_{rise}| + |A_{fall}|} + \frac{|D_{rise}| - |D_{fall}|}{2|D_{rise}| + |D_{fall}|}$$

6 Prosodic characteristics of the standard Croatian language

The core of the most European languages makes the accented syllable in a stressed word of the intonation unit, while in Croatian the core is comprised of the accented syllable and syllable behind the accented syllable because of the differentiation of the ascending and descending stress.

In Croatian, there are six different intonation cores: descending (\\), ascending (/), descending-ascending (V), descending-ascending-descending or reversed (\\ / \\), ascending and descending or complex (/ + \\) and flat (-). Their distribution is not related to the grammatical syntactic types (Babić 1991).

The most common intonation beginning in Croatian is descending, after which any type of intonation core can follow. The intonation ending is always descending or low and flat except after a flat core, when it is high and flat. If the end of intonation core is low, intonation ending extends into a flat, low tone.

Syllables in the standard Croatian can be accented or unaccented, long or short and high or low (tone). In one spoken word, only one accented syllable is allowed in Croatian. The most common accented syllable is the first syllable of the word (in about 66 % of the words in the text), then the second (in about 23 % of the words), the third (6.7 %) and the fourth (1.6 %) (Babić 1991).

Only one syllable in a spoken word is accented and all others are unaccented. Before the accented syllable all syllables are of high tone and short, and after of low tone and short or long.

Long accented syllables are 50 % longer then long unaccented syllables and short accented are 30 % longer then short unaccented syllables (Babić 1991).

Prosodic structure is an aspect of a prosody, which refers to the fact that some words group together and some have a break or natural pause between them. At the boundaries between prosodic phrases we often hear a change in the rhythm of the speech or a pause. Prosodic unit smaller than prosodic phrase and greater than phonological word is called clitic group or "spoken word". It consists of a word and proclitic or enclitic. A clitic is a morpheme that is grammatically independent, but phonologically dependent on another word (e.g. /ùškoli/). In Croatian low tone accent can only be found on the first syllable of a word and when there is a proclitic in front of a word the accent moves from the first syllable in a word to the proclitic. If a word had three or more syllables, the accent stays on the first syllable of a word (Babić 1991).

7 Related work for languages cognate to Croatian

The Slovenian language is by prosodic characteristics similar to Croatian. Several studies regarding prosody implementation into TTS have been conducted for Slovene. Šef and Gams (Šef 2003) developed a prosody generating system for TTS. They used the approach of duration modelling at two levels: intrinsic (type of voice, the voice environment, record type, syllable emphasis, etc.) and extrinsic (speed of pronunciation, position of the words within phrases and the number of syllables in a word). In F0 modelling, they differ two main phases: text segmentation on intonation units and definition of F0 contours for specific intonation units. Šef in (Šef 2006) also explored the automatic accentuation of words for Slovene words. First, it was determined whether each vowel is stressed or unstressed, and then the accents were corrected using decision trees, and taken into account the number of accented vowels and word length. Marinčič et al. (Marinčič 2009) analysed the automatic accentuation in the Slovene language, and compared human and machine capacity of accent allocation. Gros (Gros 1997) recorded a long continuous speech database and studied the influence of speech rate on the duration of syllables and phonemes. She presented models of intonation for the Slovenian language, based on the intrinsic level (word level) and extrinsic level (level higher than word level).

The Czech language can to some extent be compared to the Croatian language in its prosodic characteristics. Romportl and Kala (Romportl 2007) described the statistical F0 modelling, intensity and duration of the Czech language. Tihelka et al. (Tihelka 2010) describe a speech synthesis system for Czech language, which includes prosodic characteristic module based on the unit selection approach.

Tihelka and Matoušek (Tihelka 2006) also incorporated phonetic transcription and prosodic rules to convert an input text to its phonetic form and to estimate its suprasegmental features in ARTIC system for Slovak. Kondelova et al. (Kondelova 2013) proposed statistical approach for prosody contour modelling based on sentence classification for the Slovak language.

Sečujski (Sečujski 2002) has developed a dictionary of accents designed for Serbian and for the Serbian speech synthesis.

8 Automatic intonation event detection for Croatian speech synthesis

A procedure for automatic intonation event detection on Croatian texts based on the Tilt model was proposed (Načinović 2011). In order to detect intonation events automatically, we chose a representative set of utterances and marked four main prosodic events (pitch accents, boundaries, connections and silences) within each utterance. Then we trained HMMs to mark events automatically on a larger set of utterances. To extract F0 features from the training set of utterances we used RAPT algorithm (Talkin 1995) as implemented in VoiceboxMatlab toolbox. The obtained F0 contours contained some noise, which we smoothed with a three point median filter. We set the F0 value to 0 Hz to represent the unvoiced segments where F0 cannot be determined and in another attempt we used linear interpolation to determine the missing values. Finally, we obtained three different F0 feature sets: raw output from the RAPT algorithm smoothed and interpolated. We parameterized the detected events with tilt parameters and generated F0 contours out of those parameters. In order to evaluate the obtained F0 contours, we compared three different F0 contours based on three models for automatic event detection, trained on raw, smoothed and interpolated F0 features to the original contour. The F0 contour synthesized using hand-labelled events was also compared with the original F0. The usual measure for F0 contour evaluation is the root mean square error (RMSE) between the original and generated F0 contour. The obtained results are shown in Table 1 and graphical comparison is shown in Figure 1.

Table 1: Root Mean Square Error values for generated F0 contours

Event label model	RMSE (Hz)
raw	25.16
smoothed	26.69
interpolated	25.57
hand-labelled	**23.11**

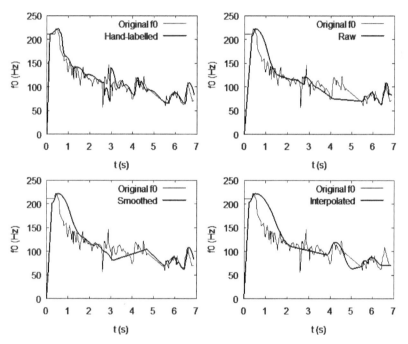

Figure 1: Comparison of the generated F0 contours with the original F0

9 Conclusion and future work

A procedure for automatic intonation event detection on Croatian texts based on the Tilt model was evaluated in terms of Root Mean Square Error values for generated F0 contours. Three different F0 feature sets: raw output from the RAPT algorithm; smoothed and interpolated were compared.

The results that we obtained are preliminary and we expect to get better results after we train the model on a larger set of sentences. All F0 contours obtained from automatically detected events have similar RMSE values, and perform comparably to the hand-labelled case, which encourages us to use this method in the future work. We plan to build CARTS for Tilt parameter prediction from text. We also plan to build a duration model for Croatian and to automatically accent the Croatian words with CARTS. Then we will incorporate the obtained duration and F0 models into Croatian TTS system and evaluate the generated speech.

List of References

Allen, Jonathan / Hunnicut, Sharon M. / Klatt, Dennis: *Text-to-Speech: The MITalk System*. Cambridge University Press: Cambridge 1987.

Aylett, Matthew: "Merging Data Driven and Rule Based Prosodic Models for Unit Selection TTS". In: Black, Alan J. / Lenzo, Kevin (eds.): *Fifth ISCA ITRW on Speech Synthesis (SSW5)*. Pitsburgh 2004, pp. 55–60, retrieved 1.3.2014., from http://www.isca-speech.org/archive_open/archive_papers/ssw5/ssw5_055.pdf.

Babić, Stjepan et al.: *Povijesni pregled, glasovi i oblici hrvatskoga književnog jezika*. Globus: Zagreb 1991.

Blin, Laurent / Miclet, Laurent: "Generating Synthetic Speech Prosody with Lazy Learning in Tree Structures". In: Cardie, Claire / Daelemans, Walter / Nedellec, Claire / Sang, Erik T. K. (eds.): *CoNLL-2000 and LLL-2000*, Lisabon 2000, pp. 87–90, retrieved 15.3.2014. from ttp://www.cnts.ua.ac.be/conll2000/pdf/08790bli.pdf.

Campbell, Nick W.: "Syllable-based segmental durations". In: Bailly, Gerard / Benoit, Christian / Sawallis, Thomas R. (eds.): *Talking Machines: Theories, Models, and Designs*, Elsevier: Amsterdam 1992, pp. 43–60.

Dusterhoff, Kurt E. / Black, Alan W. / Taylor, Paul: "Using Decision Trees within the Tilt Intonation Model to Predict f0 Contours." In: *Proceesings of Eurospeech '99*, Budapest 1999, pp. 1627–1630.

Fordyce, Cameron S. / Ostendorf, Mari: "Prosody Prediction for Speech Synthesis Using Transormational Rule-Based Learning". In: Mannell, Robert H. / Robert-Ribes, Jordi (eds.): *ICSPL-1998*, ASSTA: Sydney 1998.

Fujisaki, Hiroya / Ohno, Sumio: "Analysis and Modeling of Fundamental Frequency Contours of English Utterances". In: Pardo, Jose M.(ed.): *Eurospeech 1995*. Madrid 1995, pp. 985–988.

Gros, Jerneja: *Samodejno tvorjenje govora iz besedil, doktorska disertacija.* (Univerza v Ljubljani). (doctoral thesis). 1997.

Hirschberg, Julia: "Pitch Accent in Context: Predicting Intonational Prominence from Text". *Artificial Intelligence*, 1995, pp. 305–340.

Huang, Xuedong / Acero, Alex / Hon, Hsiao-Wuen: *Spoken Language Processing: A Guide to Theory, Algorithm and System Development.* Prentice Hall: New Jersey 2001.

Kato, Hiroaki / Tsuzaki, Minoru / Sagisaka, Yoshinori: "Acceptability for Temporal Modification of Single Vowel Segments in Isolated Words". *Journal of the Acoustical Society of America 104(1)*, 1998, pp. 540–549.

Kondelova, Anna / Toth, Jan / Gregor, Rozinaj: "Statistical Approach for Prosody Contour Modeling Based on Sentence Classification". *Elektrorevue 4(2)*, 2013, pp. 40–44.

Marinčič, Domen / Tušar, Tea / Gams, Matjaž / Šef, Tomaž: "Analysis of Automatic Stress Assignment in Slovene". *Informatica 20 (1)*, 2009, pp. 35–50.

Meron, J. "Prosodic Unit Selection Using an Imitation Speech Database". In: *4th ISCA Workshop on Speech Synthesis (SSW-4)*. Pertshire, Scotland 2001, pp. 53–57.

Načinović, Lucia et al.: "Automatic Intonation Event Detection Using Tilt Model for Croatian Speech Synthesis". In: *Information Sciences and e-Society*. Zagreb 2011. pp. 383–391.

Ostendorf, Mari / Veileux, Nanette M.: "A Hierarchical Stochastic Model for Automatic Prediction of Prosodic Boundary Location". *Computational Linguistics*, 1994, pp. 27–54.

Pierrehumbert, Janet: "Synthesizing intonation". *Journal of the Acoustical Society of America*, 1981, pp. 985–995.

Rojc, Matej et al.: "Training the tilt intonation model using the JEMA methodology". In: *Eurospeech 2005*. Lisboa 2005, pp. 3273–3276.

Romportl, Jan / Kala, Jiri: "Prosody Modelling in Czech Text-to-Speech Synthesis". In: *Proceedings of the 6th ISCA Workshop on Speech Synthesis*. Bonn 2007, pp. 200–205.

Ross, Kenneth N. / Ostendorf, Mari: "Prediction of abstract prosodic labels for speech synthesis". *Computer Speech and Language 10 (3)*, 1996, pp. 155–185.

Sečujski, Milan: "Akcenatski rečnik srpskog jezika namenjen sintezi govora na osnovu teksta". In: *DOGS2002*. Bečej 2002, pp. 17–20.

Silverman, Kim et al.: "TOBI: A Standard Scheme for Labeling Prosody". In: *Proceedings of the 1992 International Conference on Spoken Language*. Banff 1992, pp. 867–870.

Stergar, Janez / Erdem, Caglayan: "Adapting Prosody in a Text-to-Speech System". In: Fuerstner, Igor (ed.): *Products and Services; from R&D to Final Solutions*. InTech: 2010, retrieved 15.4.2014, from http://cdn.intechopen.com/pdfs-wm/12335.pdf.

Šef, Tomaž: "Automatic Accentuation of Words for Slovenian TTS System". In: Demiralp, Metin / Ahan, Aydin / Mastorakis, Nikos (eds.): *Proceedings of the 5th WSEAS International Conference on Signal Processing*. WSEA: Stevens Point, Wisconsin 2006, pp. 155–160.

Šef, Tomaž / Gams, Matjaž: "SPEAKER (GOVOREC): A Complete Slovenian Text-to Speech System". *INTERNATIONAL JOURNAL OF SPEECH TECHNOLOGY 6*, 2003, pp. 277–287.

Talkin, D.: "A robust algorithm for pitch tracking (RAPT)". In: Kleijn, W. B. / Paliwal, K. K. (eds.): *Speech coding and synthesis*. Elsevier Science B.V.: 1995, pp. 495–518.

Taylor, Paul / Black, Alan B.: "Assigning Phrase Breaks from Part-of-Speech Sequences". *Computer Speech and Language (1998) 12*, 1998, pp. 99–117.

Taylor, Paul: "Analysis and Synthesis of Intonation using the Tilt Model". *Journal of the Acoustical Society of America 107 (3)*, 2000, pp. 1697–1714.

The Centre for Speech Technology Research, The University of Edinburgh: *The Festival Speech Synthesis System*, retreived 15.4.2014., from http://www.cstr.ed.ac.uk/projects/festival/.

Taylor, Paul / Black, Alan W.: "CHATR: a generic speech synthesis system". In: *COLING '94* Proceedings of the 15th conference on Computational linguistics – Volume 2. Association for Computational Linguistics: Stroudsburg 1994, pp. 983–986.

Tihelka, Daniel / Kala, Jiri / Mtousek, Jindrich: "Enhancements of viterbi search for fast unit selection synthesis". In: *Interspeech 2010*. ISCA: 2010, pp. 174–177.

Tihelka, Daniel / Jindrich Matoušek / and Jan Romportl: "Current state of Czech text-to-speech system ARTIC". In: Text, Speech and Dialogue. 9th International Conference, TSD 2006, Brno, Czech Republic, September 11–15, 2006. Proceedings. Springer: Berlin, Heidelberg 2006, pp. 439–446.

van Santen, Jan: "Segmental Duration and Speech Timing". *Computing Prosody*, 1997, pp. 225–250.

van Santen, Jan: "Assignment of Segmental Duration in Text-to-Speech Synthesis". *Computer Speech and Language*, 1994, pp. 95–128.

Uroš Mesojedec[1,2], Zoran Levnajić[1]
(1) Faculty of Information Studies, Novo mesto, Slovenia
(2) T-media LLC, Novo mesto, Slovenia

Path to cloud-native applications, opportunities and challenges

Abstract: As an exciting new-shared platform, cloud computing represents the future of information technology. Success of the cloud computing is dependent on the availability of the adequate applications. Benefits of using computing cloud lies in specialised applications, developed with cloud in mind from the start. We devote this paper to analysing the state-of-the-art in the development of "cloud-native" applications. We present the benefits and challenges of cloud for novel approaches to application development. With the proper use of the proven software design patterns, new breed of loosely coupled cloud applications with accessible user interfaces and enormous back-end processing power can be enabled. From this can benefit even existing powerful software tools like GraphCrunch2, whose case of "cloudification" we study in more detail.

Keywords: cloud computing, software application, patterns, network analysis

1 Introduction

Cloud computing (or "the cloud" for short) is internet-based computing characterized by networking remote resources in order to allow for optimal computing accessibility and centralized data storage. This enables the users to have online need-based allocation of large-scale computer services and computing resources. The concept of sharing the resources to achieve coherence and economies of scale is similar to the concept of utility (such as power grid). For example, a cloud facility that serves European users during European business hours with a specific application, may reallocate the same resources to serve North American users during North America's business hours with a different application, thus optimizing the resources. The term "cloud" is a metaphor of resources being available but hidden from the user 'in the cloud' (see Figure 1).

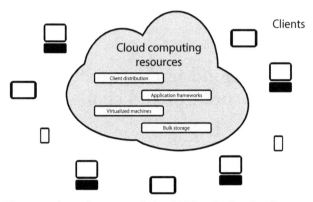

Figure 1 The metaphor of resources being hidden 'in the cloud'.

Given our increasing everyday dependence on IT services, this novel evolution of computer technology might have an enormous and global impact (Aljabre 2012). Like the Web has transformed means of communication and doing business, its technological underpinnings are beginning to emerge as an alternative to in-house IT systems. Not just the technology progress, but also new business models play a key role in propelling this new way of using IT infrastructure. Cloud enables a big scale, parallel processing of very large data sets for everyone with access to Internet. It in general requires no initial investments in expensive equipment, but rather relies on the established and proven cloud infrastructure, available for (increasingly cheap) rent. Non-cloud systems are the responsibility of the organisation itself, which is rarely adequately equipped for complex IT tasks. Their own systems are therefore complicated to design and maintain. Moreover, they usually have many other disadvantages such as not scaling well, which encourages organizations to switch to cloud as much as possible (Youseff et al 2008).

On the front of the personal users, cloud approach increasingly gains ground, as photos and music are easier to keep online than offline. In fact, even a superficial look at the current popular application landscape reveals a range of cloud-first applications that are enormously popular (McKendrick 2013). One such example is Dropbox (Drago et al 2012), file synchronisation utility, which allows keeping files online (for free up to certain size) – its core purpose is actually enabled by cloud. It is a cleanly separated client/

server application; with clients for many popular platforms and cloud back-end that enables quick and easy synchronised storage. It is worth mentioning that Dropbox is running on Amazon's cloud infrastructure, meaning that even the company itself took advantage of the cloud business model and avoided building its own cloud.

The basic technical idea of cloud is leasing the resources, which are provided as a general utility (Mell, Grance 2011). Cloud also redefines the roles of service provider into more specific infrastructure providers at the base and service providers on top. Several compelling features make cloud attractive: no up-front investment, lower operating costs, high scalability, easy access, reduction of business risks and maintenance costs. As with any new platform, overall success of the cloud is dependent on the availability of the right applications. There are benefits and trade-offs of using traditional applications in the cloud, but the real potential appears to be the employment of specialised applications and software, developed and adjusted particularly for cloud usage from the beginning.

The key focus of this paper is the analysis of the current stage of the development of exactly those kinds of applications, which we term "cloud-native" applications, since they were never designed nor intended for usage outside cloud. We will present and discuss the benefits of the cloud environment and its efficient use for a novel approach to application development, done by using proven software development patterns combined with cloud advantages. Finally, we will specifically discuss the example of currently non-cloud application called GraphCrunch (a tool for scientific network analysis of biological data) (Milenković et al 2008) and pinpoint the advantages of its "cloudification" and ultimate conversion into a cloud-native application.

2 Cloud Environment

Services supporting our daily lives and improving its comfort evolve and have always evolved in parallel with our societies. We can hardly imagine modern life without the utility services such as running water, electricity, telecommunications or heating. With improvement of the standard of living, particularly in the Western countries, this list has been growing over the past decades, to eventually include Internet. With the expanding presence of IT in essentially all aspects of human activity, its absence becomes as unthinkable as the absence of any other utility from the list. There is in fact a growing need to organise the IT services to be exactly as yet another *utility*, simply available everywhere to everyone (Buyya et al 2009). Recent developments in IT are converging to this goal, with cloud as the main proponent (Foster et al 2008), (Rappa 2004).

Let us draw some parallels to a well-known utility. We all rely on a constant and high quality supply of electric energy. Immediately upon their invention, electric power plants used direct current, which forced their positioning close to the consumers. The invention of alternating current enabled long distance transfers of electric power with the transformer as key technology enabling it. This eventually allowed modern usage of electric power, whose key advantage is robustness to distance and involvement of the end user (consumer). History of electric power usage is largely analogous to what is expected to become the history of computing services, of which the Internet is a prime example. As transformers enable voltage conversions and utilization of the long distance transfer of energy, so are the routers enabling connection of local networks to the Internet. Eventually, the cloud is expected to allow for the same kind of robustness to the Internet usage, similar to that reached by the electric power grids.

Cloud can be seen as an easy to use computing resource that we either rent or build. Ubiquitous network infrastructure enables users to easily access and utilise these resources without the need for deeper understanding of cloud inner workings and its maintenance. Applications can therefore be easier to use and with more processing power. In particular, the web interface was proven to be very approachable and easy to use in a range of practical scenarios. On the other hand, regardless of their expertise in certain fields (science, medicine etc.), some users still lack the skills needed to efficiently utilize a specific powerful software package. Cloud has the potential to alleviate this and enable a wide and easy use of powerful software for everyone. This can in turn allow for a wider range of people to use Internet for their business and personal needs, regardless of their age, education level or knowledge of (foreign) languages.

Cloud computing systems transfer the responsibility of designing, running and maintaining arbitrarily complex IT systems to the outside party and allows regular users to easily use its applications, most commonly through a simple web browser. The user has no knowledge and no worries about the issues related to maintenance of these systems, which enables him/her to enjoy the benefits of large computing power in the background cloud, accessed via simplified interfaces. On the back-end, cloud systems maintenance benefits from the economies of scale. Successful cloud providers are able to offer better service for less cost by providing specialised service for multitude of customers. They are in position to optimise all resources, from the electric power to the computing itself. Also, these systems are built to be fault tolerant and easy to maintain with automated recovery processes. Highly qualified maintenance teams are able to quickly solve potentially very complicated disruptions of services. It is very expensive for a non-cloud organisation to have such an expertise available in-house, which even if affordable, would be mostly underutilised.

There are many technical definitions of what cloud computing is or consists of. In (Zhang et al 2010) we find a layered model of cloud computing architecture (see Figure 2). It is structured into hardware, infrastructure, platforms and application layer, with different service models also being visible. At the lower end, both hardware and infrastructure layer, which include bare metal resources and also their virtualization, can be exposed as an Infrastructure as a Service (IaaS). Above that, platform layer, including development frameworks, can be exposed as a Platform as a Service (PaaS). Even higher, application layer with finalized, user-friendly interfaces can be exposed a Software as a Service (SaaS). Such architecture is modular and loosely coupled, which enables each layer to evolve on its own. All these different layers of exposure shield the user from the technicalities and finer details of the providers' technical solutions.

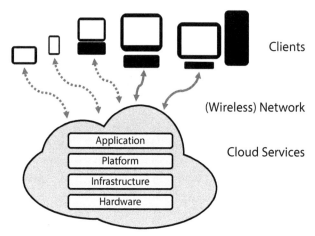

Figure 2 Illustration of the cloud system layers defining its architecture.

Using cloud services at the top layer of cloud architecture (SaaS) usually requires only a web browser. After years of competition among the browsers ('browser wars'), the prevalence of widely used software services enabled informal common functionality specification, which majority of web browser providers are required to supply without hindrance of proprietary enhancements and browser-specific bugs. Usage patterns strongly preferred the open web (West, Mace 2010).

What we observed at the SaaS level is also a necessity for all other exposures, if they want to reach the utility status. Looking at the PaaS level, there are cloud resources, exposed at a platform, which can be programmed into automated solutions. If we want to achieve utility status of cloud even at this level, some common programming frameworks should be available and as such would represent independent clients, which would enable the largest audience to participate on every cloud platform available. Embracing open standards, especially in cloud computing, which was enabled with open Internet protocols, is better long-term strategy, not only for users, but also for providers. Innovation happens above the common standardised platform and is available to a largest audience possible.

Software development is also affected by the cloud proliferation. There are different models to utilise the cloud for software applications. It is possible to host certain types of "traditional" applications (mostly) unmodified.

In this scenario we only gain infrastructural benefits of a cloud system. On the other hand, cloud-native applications can gain all of the benefits of such systems. Cloud-native application should be written for the platform layer of cloud service and should be aware and actively use cloud specific services, such as high-speed connectivity, abundant processing resources and storage capacity on demand. These features are commonly not available for non-cloud applications, making cloud-native applications inherently novel and different.

3 Cloud Applications and the Process of Cloudification

Standard architectural patterns are commonly used in the development of any new software. As these development projects are usually complex, following the proven scheme of patterns can relieve some of the inherent risks of such endeavours and possibly facilitate the task of developers. Any developer wants to efficiently manage the complexity of all of the software parts, including those that we rely on every day.

Model View Controller (MVC) (Reenskaug 1978), (Krasner 1988) is one of the most successful architectural patterns, with a huge impact on software engineering since its introduction in the late 1970's. Its main purpose is to establish a clear separation between the building blocks of the completed software project. The peculiarity of MVC pattern scheme is that it fits nicely into the cloud paradigm, because it clearly separates the building block that faces the user (called 'View') from the data structures in the back-end (termed 'Model'). It also integrates two of them into a cohesive unity by connecting them through another block (called 'Controller', see Figure 3). These three blocks have their natural counterparts in the cloud system. Web interface corresponds to the View, Model is analogous to the data storage, while the Controller is the software 'glue' running in the platform layer of a given cloud environment. A variety of software projects that pre-date cloud successfully relied on MVC pattern. Yet its real benefits can perhaps be best exploited when employed to develop the cloud applications, in particular cloud-native applications. We could say that MVC is one of the better approaches in cloudification of existing applications. There are existing applications, which utilize the MVC pattern in other paradigms, e.g. desktop software with graphical user interface. For such applications the task of cloudification is made easier since they already employ the separation in application logic (by the MVC pattern) that is necessary for successful porting into the cloud paradigm.

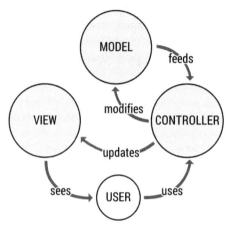

Figure 3 Schematics of elements and interactions in the MVC architectural pattern.

Clear separation between the data, processing logic, and the presentation is a natural state of any cloud application. Data is available from different sources, usually accessible through the resource location, for instance uniform resource locator (URL) address. This represents the Model of our pattern. In our pattern the processing of the data is done by the Controller. Controllers in the cloud environment are commonly running in virtualised computing resources in a datacentre. To manage the application environment and present the results of a Controller we need the View. Progress of the web technologies enabled almost any view to be implemented as a web application. Therefore we can use arbitrary complex cloud application just through the web interface, which is available on almost any networked device, from the desktop personal computers to the mobile smartphones. Employing the MVC pattern is therefore almost natural way of building cloud-native applications, which are loosely coupled, client-independent (Mesojedec 2013), very powerful, and at the same time open to further collaboration (Manjunatha et al 2010).

We take a closer look to an example of a successful cloud application. One of the most commonly used pieces of software is a simple spread sheet, interactive cross-calculated table, allowing to easily write and use a table with numbers or words. Historical examples of a desktop spread sheets are VisiCalc, Lotus 1-2-3, and in the recent years most commonly known Microsoft Excel. Upgrading such application in the cloud was no easy task, but current solutions not only caught up with the capabilities of for example desktop versions, but also have surpassed them on many levels.

There are many widely known benefits of cloud approach, e.g. users can access its data form many clients, collaboration is easier etc. Direct benefits of employing the MVC pattern are also evident. Efficient large-scale data processing is possible, since the Model can be utilized by any (big) data repository somewhere else in the cloud and the Controller has many (virtualized) processor cores in the cloud data centre. Cost of infrastructure needed for large scale processing is minimised through cloud model, as we don't have to invest up front in the equipment capable of handling peak loads but we only rent such capabilities when needed. Also, simplified user interface through web based views enables even non-experts in the field to efficiently use most of the application capabilities. Therefore, clearly separated cloud spread sheet (Herrick, 2009) by the MVC pattern has a central data model, which is the same for all of the clients and users. This means that collaboration is part of the pattern on which application was build. It can support simultaneous edits of many users, who can comment and interactively cooperate on the data. The entire history of edits is stored, allowing reverting to any past version, should any date become lost in the process. It becomes straightforward to use any URL-accessible data and import it into our calculations or use it while it updates in real time. Example of such multi-user spread sheet can be readily accessed for free via Google Drive, for instance. Cloud capabilities are already in this respect an order of magnitude greater than that of any desktop class system. Finally, progress in web technologies made possible to develop very user-friendly view options, thus making the view practically equivalent to the simple web browser.

4 Large Network Analysis

We live in the age of Big Data, where increasing accumulation of new data call for new approaches in analysing them. Networks (graphs) are powerful mathematical framework, which allow us to elegantly represent and study complex systems and in general complex datasets. Complex systems on the other hand, can be found on all scales in nature and in society, ranging from information, social, physical, transportation, and biological systems. Among many different types of biological networks, protein-protein interaction (PPI) are possibly the most interesting, where proteins within cell are represented as nodes, while their chemical interactions are modelled as links. The network analysis software GraphCrunch 2 (GC2) is a tool that implements the latest research on biological network analysis; in particular PPI networks (Kuchaiev et al 2011). It is a substantial upgrade of original GraphCrunch which implements the most used random network models and compares them to the data networks, analysing specific network properties. GC2 also implements GRAph ALigner (GRAAL) algorithm for topological network alignment, which can expose large, contiguous, dense regions of topological and functional similarities. In this regard GRAAL surpasses any other existing tool. GC2 is already a very efficient and useful tool, even for experts without extensive knowledge of networks and network modelling (see Table 1).

Table 1　Comparison of software tools for biological network analysis, table source (Kuchaiev et al 2011).

Software package	Graph properties	# of models	Graphlets	Visualization	Clustering	GNA
GraphCrunch 2	Yes	7	Yes	Yes (Results)	Yes	Yes
GraphCrunch	Yes	5	Yes	Yes (Results)	No	No
Cytoscape	Yes	6	Limited	Yes	Yes	No
Visant	Yes	1	No	Yes	No	No
mFinder	No	3	No	Yes (mDraw)	No	No
MAVisto	No	1	No	Yes	No	No
FANMOD	No	3	No	Yes	No	No
tYNA	Yes	0	No	Yes	No	No
pajek	Yes	2	No	Yes	Yes	No
IsoRank	No	0	No	No	No	Yes
Graemlin	No	0	No	No	No	Yes
GraphM	No	0	No	No	No	Yes

However, GC2 could benefit even more from the cloudification. The challenges for further advancement of GC2 capabilities and its wider use can be efficiently addressed by porting the application into the cloud environment. By using the MVC, as mentioned above, pattern separation of application modules large community of network experts, users from other science domains and also software developers can be engaged on different levels. Also, cloud environment will enable easier use of large data models, available through URL. Cloud datacentre capabilities can drastically expand software tool computing power without the need for up-front investments in hardware. If large processing power is required for especially complex network analysis, it can simply be rented for a reasonable price, driven lower every day through harsh competitive ecosystem of different cloud providers (Ograph, Morgens 2008). Clear separation of application modules through the MVC model could also expand GC2 popularity with developer community. For example, as software is open sourced, experts in the web interface domain could be engaged to provide just View plug-ins, without even handling internal Controller logic with raw network analysis capabilities. The same can be said for network experts, which can provide Controller expansion, without the need of interacting with the view parts.

We should not forget the social component of cloud available software. Collaboration is made much easier. For example results can be shared simply by emailing the URL of the specific View. This opens great opportunities of further analysis, discussion and expansion of results by using all of the popular social tools. Cloud also encourages real-time collaboration (Graham 2011). Many experts can work on the same Model simultaneously, either through different Views or even using the same View if their research is tied.

5 Public Cloud Providers

As cloud is gaining recognition and acceptance in the scientific and business communities, few models for comparing cloud providers performance have been established (Li et al 2010), (Ueda, Nakatani 2010). They mostly focus on the raw performance and network capabilities. When we are interested in developing cloud native applications or porting existing application into cloud ('cloudification'), different measurements of cloudification quality would be more useful. Evaluating cloud platforms as a suitable environment for application development is a field of current research and new useful models are yet to be published. Work is that more challenging because cloud software development is still a young field and in constant mutability as proven software architectures and patterns need to be adapted to the current state of the cloud which is rapidly evolving. Nevertheless, some core measures and capabilities are clear indicators of cloud platform's development facilities (Dillon et al 2010).

Performance metrics (Li et al 2010) needs to be considered, since they are important for the capability and usability of the final product. Unfortunately, they do not tell as much about the development proficiencies. In most cases, cloud platforms limit our choice of programming language and supported software frameworks. If our existing investment in the code is strongly correlated to the chosen programming language and/or software frameworks, our choices are either limited or we have to take the cost of porting or even reengineering existing codebase to a new language into consideration.

As cloud is developing, developer friendliness is becoming the important cloud differentiator and an area of fierce competition between providers. As any new computing platform, cloud is also critically dependent on the developer acceptance and availability of native applications, which can propel its popularity and wider use. We can reasonably expect for all the leading providers to embrace as large developer community as possible and provide efficient tools for cloud software development, including support for popular languages and proven architectures as MVC we presented here.

6 Disussion and Conclusions

We have presented the benefits of a cloud environment for a novel approach to application development. Cloud has a large potential to revolutionize not only IT architectures but also software development patterns and application usage.

Cloud has the right potential to enable global computing infrastructure as another utility service. But it is reliant on other infrastructure. It is obvious that it needs electric power, which although it is not globally available, is a common utility service. Also mobile, specifically battery technology can alleviate some of the issues of using cloud applications in areas with not such reliable power sources. Another crucial infrastructure technology for cloud is the fast and reliable telecommunication network. This is an area of large interest of cloud businesses, because the majority of human population still cannot enjoy broadband connectivity. We can reasonably expect this situation to improve drastically in the upcoming years.

With the proper use of the proven architectural patterns, such as the MVC pattern, we can enable new breed of loosely coupled cloud applications with accessible user interfaces and enormous back end processing power, which is available from the cloud datacentres. This opens the path for solving the entirely new class of problems and also enables easier collaboration and knowledge sharing.

This can be demonstrated on the specific example of porting existing powerful application, like GraphCrunch 2, into the cloud paradigm. Even without functional expansion, there are many benefits of porting it to the cloud. With the port available, there are many further possibilities of expanding application functionality and also larger and easier use, collaboration and sharing of the research results.

References

Wikipedia: *Cloud Computing*, retrieved September 2014 from http://en.wikipedia.org/wiki/Cloud_computing.

Aljabre, A.: "Cloud computing for increased business value". *International Journal of Business and Social Science*, 3(1), 2012, pp. 234–239.

Youseff, L. / Butrico, M. / Da Silva, D.: "Toward a unified ontology of cloud computing". *Grid Computing Environments Workshop*, 2008. GCE'08 IEEEE, pp. 1–10

McKendrick, J.: "20 Most Popular Cloud-Based Apps Downloaded into Enterprises". Forbes.com, April 2013, retrieved September 2014 from http://www.forbes.com/sites/joemckendrick/2013/03/27/20-most-popular-cloud-based-apps-downloaded-into-enterprises/.

Drago, I., et al.: "Inside dropbox: understanding personal cloud storage services", Proceedings of the 2012 ACM conference on Internet measurement conference, 2012, pp. 481–494.

Mell, P. / Grance, T.: "Cloud Computing Synopsis and Recommendations". NIST Special Publication 800–146, National Institute of Standards and

Technology, U.S. Department of Commerce, May 2011, retrieved September 2014 from http://csrc.nist.gov/publications/drafts/800–146/ Draft-NIST-SP800-146.pdf.

Milenković, T. / Lai, J. / Pržulj, N.: "Graphcrunch: a tool for large network analyses", BMC bioinformatics, 9(1), 2008.

Buyya, R. / Yeo, C. S. / Venugopal, S. et al.: "Cloud computing and emerging IT platforms: Vision, hype, and reality for delivering computing as the 5th utility". Future Generation computer systems, 25(6), 2009, pp. 599–616.

Foster, I. / Zhao, Y. / Raicu, I. / Lu, S.: "Cloud computing and grid computing 360-degree compared", Grid Computing Environments Workshop, GCE'08, 2008, pp. 1–10.

Rappa, M. A.: "The utility business model and the future of computing services", IBM Systems Journal, 43(1), 2004, pp. 32–42.

Zhang, Q. / Cheng, L. / Boutaba, R.: "Cloud computing: state-of-the-art and research challenges", Journal of Internet Services and Applications, 1(1), 2010, pp. 7–18.

West, J. / Mace, M.: "Browsing as the killer app: Explaining the rapid success of Apple's iPhone", Telecommunications Policy, 34(5), 2010, pp. 270–286.

Reenskaug, T.: "The Original MVC Reports". Xerox Palo Alto Research Laboratory, PARC, 1978.

Krasner, G.E. / Pope, S.T.: "A description of the model-view-controller user interface paradigm in the smalltalk-80 system", Journal of object oriented programming 1.3, 1988, pp. 26–49.

Burbeck, S.: "Applications Programming in Smalltalk-80: How to Use Model-View-Controller (MVC)". Softsmarts, Inc., 1987, retrieved September 2014 from http://st-www.cs.illinois.edu/users/smarch/st-docs/ mvc.html.

Mesojedec, U.: "Client-Independence as the Critical Step Towards a New Level of Cloud Computing", Proceedings of the 7th European Computing Conference (ECC'13), Dubrovnik, Croatia, June 25–27, 2013, (Recent Advances in Computer Engineering Series, 13). WSEAS Press, cop. 2013, pp. 179–184.

Manjunatha, A. / Ranabahu, A. / Sheth, A. et al.: "Power of Clouds In Your Pocket: An Efficient Approach for Cloud Mobile Hybrid Application

Development". 2nd IEEE International Conference on Cloud Computing Technology and Science, IEEE, 2010, pp. 496–503.

Wikipedia: Spreadsheet, retrieved September 2014 from http://en.wikipedia. org/wiki/Spreadsheet.

Herrick, D. R.: "Google this!: using Google apps for collaboration and productivity", Proceedings of the 37th annual ACM SIGUCCS fall conference, 2009, pp. 55–64.

Kuchaiev, O. / Stevanović, A. / Hayes, W. et al.: "GraphCrunch 2: software tool for network modeling, alignment and clustering". BMC bioinformatics, 12(1), 24, 2011.

Ograph, B. T. / Morgens, Y.R.: "Cloud computing". Communications of the ACM 51.7, 2008.

Graham, M.: "Cloud collaboration: Peer-production and the engineering of the internet". Engineering earth. Springer Netherlands, 2011, pp. 67–83.

Li, A. / Yang, X. / Kandula, S. et al.: "CloudCmp: comparing public cloud providers". Proceedings of the 10th ACM SIGCOMM conference on Internet measurement, 2010, pp. 1–14.

Ueda, Y. / Nakatani, T.: "Performance variations of two open-source cloud platforms". Workload Characterization (IISWC), IEEE International Symposium, 2010, pp. 1–10.

Dillon, T. / Wu, C. / Chang, E.: "Cloud computing: issues and challenges". Advanced Information Networking and Applications (AINA), 24th IEEE International Conference, 2010, pp. 27–33.

Google: Project *Loon*, retrieved September 2014 from http://www.google. com/loon/.

www.ingramcontent.com/pod-product-compliance
Lightning Source LLC
LaVergne TN
LVHW052301060326
832902LV00021B/3653